The Little Book
of
WAR
POEMS

The Little Book
of

WAR
POEMS

Edited by
NICK DE SOMOGYI

This is a Parragon Book
This edition published in 2005

Parragon
Queen Street House
4 Queen Street
Bath BA1 1HE, UK

Copyright © Parragon 2001

This book was created by Magpie Books,
an imprint of Constable & Robinson Ltd

Cover image courtesy of Getty Images
Cover by Talking Design

ISBN 1-40546-128-4

A copy of the British Library Catedoguing-in-Publication Data
is available from the British Library

Printed in China

Contents

❧

Introduction

Sophocles long ago
Heard it on the Ægean and it brought
Into his mind the turbid ebb and flow
Of human misery.
>> Matthew Arnold, *Dover Beach*

War has often been called a tragedy. It has also been noticed that a battle obeys the so-called Three Unities of classical drama, first observed by Aristotle long ago. Like a tragedy by Sophocles, the events of a battle are restricted to a limited period of time, often a single day; they are played out in a single, defined space; and the action is centered upon a single objective. Even today, the language of war seems to remember the poetic stage: international dialogues are held and worst-case scenarios plotted; campaigns are waged in theaters of war, by soldiers organized into units called companies. And just as actors perfect their roles in full dress rehearsals, so soldiers in uniform perfect their duties in army maneuvers. These days we even watch our wars live on television.

The war poems in this collection are organized into five sections, like the five acts of a classical tragedy. Each section is named after a military command, in honor of the many poets included here who themselves saw active service. The following pages advance from the onset of war ("Forward March"), via the eve of battle ("Who Goes There?"), to the catastrophe of the Front Line ("Charge!"); then return, with the veterans, to the fears and uncertainties of the Home Front ("Stand at Ease"); and close at last in the aftermath of remembrance ("Fall Out").

But the poets gathered here, amid Arnold's "turbid ebb and flow | Of human misery", are not all tragic ones, not even all gloomy ones. Their voices are as varied as the weather or the sea that they so often describe. They carry exhortation, indignation, and resignation; they speak in elegy and epic; and they often even make us laugh. Perhaps not all their poems tell the truth about war; but each poem adds its voice to the forum of debate in which, two and a half millennia ago, Tragedy was born.

Aristotle considered that Tragedy cleanses our spirits by the emotions it evokes in us of pity and fear. Many of the poems that follow may act in a similar way, and (in

Donne's words) "breed a just true fear" in us, "a mingled sense" (in Wordsworth's) "Of fear and sorrow":

> For by my glee might many men have laughed,
> And of my weeping something had been left,
> Which must die now. I mean the truth untold
> The pity of war, the pity war distilled.
>
> Wilfred Owen, *Strange Meeting*

Chapter 1

~

FORWARD MARCH

We start on the beach, that point of no return, that line in the sand where, throughout history, conscripts and volunteers have been transformed into soldiers as they embark for service overseas. The rhythm of the drum beats through many of these poems. "Soldiers, prepare!" . . . "Farewell, adieu" . . . "Let us go" . . .

from The Ballad of Agincourt

Fair stood the wind for France,
When we our sails advance,
Nor now to prove our chance
    Longer will tarry;
But putting to the main,
At Caux, the mouth of Seine,
With all his martial train,
    Landed King Harry.

And taking many a fort,
Furnished in warlike sort,
Marcheth towards Agincourt
    In happy hour;
Skirmishing day by day,
With those that stopped his way,
Where the French general lay,
    With all his power.

Which, in his height of pride
King Henry to deride,
His ransom to provide
    To the king sending.

Which he neglects the while,
As from a nation vile,
Yet, with an angry smile,
    Their fall portending.

And turning to his men,
Quoth our brave Henry then,
"Though they to one be ten,
    Be not amazed.
Yet have we well begun,
Battles so bravely won
Have ever to the sun
    By fame been raised."

Michael Drayton (1563–1631)

Embarcation

~

Here, where Vespasian's legions struck the sands,
And Cerdic with his Saxons entered in,
And Henry's army leapt afloat to win
Convincing triumphs over neighbour lands,

Vaster battalions press for further strands,
To argue in the selfsame bloody mode
Which this late age of thought, and pact, and code,
Still fails to mend. – Now deckward tramp the bands,

Yellow as autumn leaves, alive as spring;
And as each host draws out upon the sea
Beyond which lies the tragical To-be,
None dubious of the cause, none murmuring,

Wives, sisters, parents, wave white hands and smile,
As if they knew not that they weep the while.

Thomas Hardy (1840–1928)

To the Men of Kent, October 1803

Vanguard of liberty, ye men of Kent!
Ye children of a soil that doth advance
Its haughty brow against the coast of France,
Now is the time to prove your hardiment!
To France be words of invitation sent!
They from their fields can see the countenance
Of your fierce war, may ken the glittering lance,
And hear you shouting forth your brave intent.
Left single, in bold parley, ye, of yore,
Did from the Norman win a gallant wreath;
Confirmed the charters that were yours before; –
No parleying now! In Britain is one breath;
We are all with you now from shore to shore: –
Ye men of Kent, 'tis victory or death!

William Wordsworth (1770–1850)

from Edward III

Death's name is much more mighty than his deeds:
Thy parcelling this power hath made it more.
As many sands as these my hands can hold
Are but my handful of so many sands:
Then, all the world — and call it but a power —
Easily ta'en up, and quickly thrown away.
But if I stand to count them sand by sand,
The number would confound my memory,
And make a thousand millions of a task,
Which briefly is no more indeed than one.
These quarters, squadrons, and these regiments,
Before, behind us, and on either hand,
Are but a power. When we name a man,
His hand, his foot, his head, hath several strengths,
And being all but one self instant strength,
Why, all this many, Audley, is but one,
And we can call it all but one man's strength.
He that hath far to go, tells it by miles;
If he should tell the steps, it kills the heart;
The drops are infinite that make a flood,
And yet, thou knowest, we call it but a rain.
There is but one France, one King of France:

That France hath no more kings, and that same king
Hath but the puissant legion of one king;
And we have one. Then apprehend no odds,
For one to one is fair equality.

Anon (c. 1590)

Ye Mariners of England

Ye mariners of England,
That guard our native seas;
Whose flag has braved, a thousand years,
The battle and the breeze!
Your glorious standard launch again
To match another foe!
And sweep through the deep,
While the stormy winds do blow;
While the battle rages loud and long,
And the stormy winds do blow.

The spirits of your fathers
Shall start from every wave! —
For the deck it was their field of fame,
And ocean was their grave:
Where Blake and mighty Nelson fell,
Your manly hearts shall glow,
As ye sweep through the deep,
While the stormy winds do blow;
While the battle rages loud and long,
And the stormy winds do blow.

Britannia needs no bulwarks,
No towers along the steep;
Her march is o'er the mountain-waves,
Her home is on the deep.
With thunders from her native oak
She quells the floods below, –
As they roar on the shore,
When the stormy winds do blow;
When the battle rages loud and long,
And the stormy winds do blow.

The meteor flag of England
Shall yet terrific burn;
Till danger's troubled night depart,
And the star of peace return.
Then, then, ye ocean warriors!
Our song and feast shall flow
To the fame of your name,
When the storm has ceased to blow;
When the fiery fight is heard no more,
And the storm has ceased to blow.

Thomas Campbell (1777–1844)

from The Pirates of Penzance

I am the very model of the modern Major-General,
I've information vegetable, animal, and mineral,
I know the kings of England, and I quote the fights
    historical,
From Marathon to Waterloo, in order categorical.

I'm very well acquainted too with matters
    mathematical,
I understand equations both the simple and
    quadratical,
About binomial theorem I'm teeming with a lot o'
    news –
With many cheerful facts about the square of the
    hypotenuse.

I'm very good at integral and differential calculus,
I know the scientific names of beings animalculous;
In short, in matters vegetable, animal, and mineral,
I am the very model of the modern Major-General.

In fact, when I know what is meant by *mamelon* and
    ravelin,
When I can tell at sight a *châssepot* rifle from a
    javelin,
When such affairs as sorties and surprises I'm more
    wary at,
And when I know precisely what is meant by
    commissariat,

When I have learnt what progress has been made in
    modern gunnery,
When I know more of tactics than a novice in a
    nunnery,
In short, when I've a smattering of elemental strategy,
You'll say a better Major-Gene*ral* has never *sat* a gee.

For my military knowledge, though I'm plucky and
    adventury,
Has only been brought down to the beginning of the
    century;
But still in matters vegetable, animal, and mineral,
I am the very model of the modern Major-General.

W. S. Gilbert (1836–1911)

from Tamburlaine, Part Two

The ditches must be deep, the counterscarps
Narrow and steep, the walls made high and broad,
The bulwarks and the rampiers large and strong,
With cavalieros and thick counterforts,
And room within to lodge six thousand men.
It must have privy ditches, countermines,
And secret issuings to defend the ditch.
It must have high argins and covered ways
To keep the bulwark fronts from battery,
And parapets to hide the musketeers;
Casemates to place the great artillery,
And store of ordnance that from every flank
May scour the outward curtains of the fort,
Dismount the cannon of the adverse part,
Murder the foe and save their walls from breach.
When this is learned for service on the land,
By plain and easy demonstration,
I'll teach you how to make the water mount,
That you may dry-foot march through lakes and
     pools,
Deep rivers, havens, creeks and little seas,
And make a fortress in the raging waves,

Fenced with the concave of a monstrous rock,
Invincible by nature of the place.
When this is done, then are ye soldiers,
And worthy sons of Tamburlaine the Great.

Christopher Marlowe (1564–93)

A War Song to Englishmen

Prepare, prepare the iron helm of war,
Bring forth the lots, cast in the spacious orb;
Th' Angel of Fate turns them with mighty hands,
And casts them out upon the darkened earth!
      Prepare, prepare.

Prepare your hearts for Death's cold hand! Prepare
Your souls for flight, your bodies for the earth!
Prepare your arms for glorious victory!
Prepare your eyes to meet a holy God!
      Prepare, prepare.

Whose fatal scroll is that? Methinks 'tis mine!
Why sinks my heart, why faltereth my tongue?
Had I three lives, I'd die in such a cause,
And rise, with ghosts, over the well-fought field.
      Prepare, prepare.

The arrows of Almighty God are drawn!
Angels of Death stand in the low'ring heavens!
Thousands of souls must seek the realms of light,
And walk together on the clouds of heaven!
     Prepare, prepare.

Soldiers, prepare! Our cause is heaven's cause;
Soldiers, prepare! Be worthy of our cause:
Prepare to meet our fathers in the sky:
Prepare, O troops, that are to fall today!
     Prepare, prepare.

                     William Blake (1757–1827)

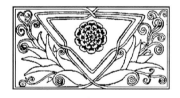

from Fears in Solitude

Thankless too for peace,
(Peace long preserved by fleets and perilous seas)
Secure from actual warfare, we have loved
To swell the war-whoop, passionate for war!
Alas! for ages ignorant of all
Its ghastlier workings (famine or blue plague,
Battle, or siege, or flight through wintry snows),
We, this whole people, have been clamorous
For war and bloodshed; animating sports,
The which we pay for as a thing to talk of,
Spectators and not combatants! No guess
Anticipative of a wrong unfelt,
No speculation on contingency,
However dim and vague, too vague and dim
To yield a justifying cause; and forth
(Stuffed out with big preamble, holy names,
And adjurations of the God in Heaven),
We send our mandates for the certain death
Of thousands and ten thousands! Boys and girls,
And women, that would groan to see a child
Pull off an insect's leg, all read of war,
The best amusement for our morning meal!

The poor wretch, who has learnt his only prayers
From curses, who knows scarcely words enough
To ask a blessing from his Heavenly Father,
Becomes a fluent phraseman, absolute
And technical in victories and defeats,
And all our dainty terms for fratricide;
Terms which we trundle smoothly o'er our tongues
Like mere abstractions, empty sounds to which
We join no feeling and attach no form!
As if the soldier died without a wound;
As if the fibres of this godlike frame
Were gored without a pang; as if the wretch,
Who fell in battle, doing bloody deeds,
Passed off to Heaven, translated and not killed;
As though he had no wife to pine for him,
No God to judge him! Therefore, evil days
Are coming on us, O my countrymen!
And what if all-avenging Providence,
Strong and retributive, should make us know
The meaning of our words, force us to feel
The desolation and the agony
Of our fierce doings?

Samuel Taylor Coleridge (1772–1834)

On Receiving News of the War

~

Snow is a strange white word;
No ice or frost
Has asked of bud or bird
For Winter's cost.

Yet ice and frost and snow
From earth to sky
This Summer land doth know;
No man knows why.

In all men's hearts it is:
Some spirit old
Hath turned with malign kiss
Our lives to mould.

Red fangs have torn His face,
God's blood is shed:
He mourns from His lone place
His children dead.

O ancient crimson curse!
Corrode, consume;
Give back this universe
Its pristine bloom.

Isaac Rosenberg (1890–1918)

from Metamorphoses

~

Then sprang up first the golden age, which of itself
  maintained
The truth and right of everything, unforced and
  unconstrained.
There was no fear of punishment, there was no
  threatening law
In brazen tables nailéd up to keep the folk in awe.
There was no man would crouch or creep to Judge,
  with cap in hand:
They livéd safe without a Judge in every realm and
  land.
The lofty pine tree was not hewn from mountains
  where it stood,
In seeking strange and foreign lands, to rove upon
  the flood.
Men knew no other countries yet than where
  themselves did keep;
There was no town encloséd yet with walls and
  ditches deep.
No horn nor trumpet was in use, no sword or helmet
  worn:

The world was such that soldiers' help might easily be
    forborn.
The fertile earth as yet was free, untouched of sword
    or plough,
And yet it yielded of itself of every thing enough.

Ovid (43 BC–18 AD)
translated by Arthur Golding (1536–1605)

War

~

Next marcheth war, break-law, and custom-breaker,
Raze-fort, spill-blood, burn-hostry, loving-tears.
Under his brazen feet stoops all the earth,
His mouth a flaming brand, his voice a thunder:
Each finger of his hand a cannon is;
And each regard of his a flaming lightning flash.
Disorder, fear, despair, and speedy flight
Do ragged march before his murdering host:
As, likewise, burning pride, impiety,
Rage, discord, sackage and impunity,
Horror and spoil, ruin and cruelty,
Eachwhere attends, where barbarous he walks,
Moan, solitude, with fear do still accost
The bloody steps of his undaunted host.

Guillaume du Bartas (1544–90)
translated by Thomas Lodge (1558–1625)

The House of Ate, *from* The Faerie Queene

~

Her name was Ate, mother of debate
  And all dissention which doth daily grow
  Amongst frail men, that many a public state
  And many a private oft doth overthrow.
  Her false Duessa, who full well did know,
  To be most fit to trouble noble knights
  Which hunt for honour, raiséd from below,
  Out of the dwellings of the damnéd sprights,
Where she in darkness wastes her curséd days and
    nights.

Hard by the gates of hell her dwelling is,
  There whereas all the plagues and harms abound,
  Which punish wicked men that walk amiss.
  It is a darksome delve far underground,
  With thorns and barren brakes environed round,
  That none the same may easily out win;
  Yet many ways to enter may be found,
  But none to issue forth when one is in:
For discord harder is to end than to begin.

And all within, the riven walls were hung
    With ragged monuments of times forepast,
    All which the sad effects of discord sung.
    There were rent robes and broken sceptres placed,
    Altars defiled, and holy things defaced,
    Disshivered spears, and shields ytorn in twain,
    Great cities ransacked, and strong castles razed,
    Nations captived, and huge armies slain:
Of all which ruins there some relics did remain.

Edmund Spenser (c. 1553–99)

from The Four Elements: Fire

∽

What is my worth, both ye and all men know:
In little time I can but little show,
But what I am, let learnéd Grecians say;
What I can do well skilled mechanics may.
The benefit all living by me find,
All sorts of artists, here declare your mind.
What tool was ever framed but by my might?
Ye Martialists, what weapons for your fight
To try your valour by, but it must feel
My force? Your sword and gun, your lance of steel –
Your cannon's bootless and your powder too
Without mine aid. Alas, what can they do?
The adverse walls not shaked, the mines not blown,
And in despite the city keeps her own.
But I, with one grenado or petard,
Set ope those gates, that 'fore so strong were barred.
Ye husbandmen, your coulters, made by me,
Your hoes, your mattocks, and whate'er you see,
Subdue the earth, and fit it for your grain
That so it might in time requite your pain:
Though strong-limbed Vulcan forged it by his skill,
I made it flexible unto his will.

Anne Bradstreet (1612–72)

∽ 35 ∽

from An Execration Upon Vulcan

Pox on your flameship, Vulcan, if it be
To all as fatal as it hath been to me
And to Paul's steeple, which was unto us
'Bove all your fireworks had at Ephesus
Or Alexandria; and though a divine
Loss, remains yet unrepaired as mine.
Would you had kept your forge at Etna still,
And there made swords, bills, glaives, and arms
    your fill,
Maintained the trade at Bilbo or elsewhere,
Struck in at Milan with the cutlers there,
Or stayed but where the friar and you first met
Who from the devil's arse did guns beget,
Or fixed in the Low Countries, where you might
On both sides do your mischiefs with delight,
Blow up and ruin, mine and countermine,
Make your petards and grenades, all your fine
Engines of murder, and receive the praise
Of massacring mankind so many ways.

                Ben Jonson (1572–1640)

from The Former Age

~

What should it have avayled to war?
There lay no profit, there was no richesse,
But curséd was the time (I dare well say)
That men first did their sweaty business,
To grub up metal, lurking in darkness,
And in rivers first gems sought.
Alas! Then sprang up all the cursedness
Of covetise, that first our sorrow brought!

Yet were no palace-chambers, ne no halls.
In caves and in woods, soft and sweet
Slepten this blesséd folk, withouten walls,
On grass or leaves in perfect quiet;
No down of feathers, ne no bleachéd sheet,
Was kid to them, but in surety they slept.
Their hearts were all one, withouten galls:
Evereach of them his faith to other kept.

Unforgéd was the hauberk and the plate.
The lambish people, void of all vice,
Hadden no fantasy to debate,
But each of them would other well cherish.

No pride, non envy, non avarice,
No lord, no taxage by no tyranny,
Humblesse and peace – good faith the empress.

Yet was not Jupiter the lecherous
(That first was father of delicacy)
Come in this world; ne Nimrod, desirous
To reign, had not made his towers high.
Alas, alas! Now may men weep and cry!
For in our days nis but covetise,
Doubleness and treason, and envy,
Poison, manslaughter, and murder in sundry wise.

Geoffrey Chaucer (1340–1400) after Ovid

from The Two Noble Kinsmen

～

Thou mighty one, that with thy power hast turned
Green Neptune into purple! Whose approach
Comets prewarn, whose havoc in vast field
Unearthed skulls proclaim! Whose breath blows
　　down
The teeming Ceres' foison! Who dost pluck
With hand armipotent from forth blue clouds
The masoned turrets! That both mak'st and break'st
The stony girths of cities! Me, thy pupil,
Youngest follower of thy drum, instruct this day
With military skill, that to thy laud
I may advance my streamer, and by thee
Be styled the lord o'th' day. Give me, great Mars,
Some token of thy pleasure.
O great corrector of enormous times,
Shaker of o'er-rank states; thou grand decider
Of dusty and old titles, that healest with blood
The earth when it is sick, and curest the world
O'th' pleurisy of people: I do take
Thy signs auspiciously, and in thy name
To my design march boldly. Let us go.

William Shakespeare (1564–1616)

from The Recruiting Serjeant

All gallant lads, who know no fears,
To the drum-head repair:
To serve the king, for volunteers,
Speak you, my boys, that dare.
Come, who'll be a grenadier?
The 'listing-money down,
Is three guineas and a crown,
To be spent in punch, in beer.

Drums strike up a flourish, and follow me now,
All honest hearts and clever;
Free quarters and beer at the sign of the Plough:
Huzza! King George for ever!

Isaac Bickerstaffe (1733?–1812)

from **Playing at Soldiers**

What little urchin is there never
Hath had that early scarlet fever,
    Of martial trappings caught?
"Trappings" well-called – because they trap
And catch full many a country chap
    To go where fields are fought!

What little urchin with a rag
Hath never made a little flag
    (Our plate will show the manner),
And wooed each tiny neighbour still,
Tommy or Harry, Dick or Will,
    To come beneath the banner!

Just like that ancient shape of mist,
In *Hamlet* crying, "List, O 'list!"
    Come, who will serve the king,
And strike frog-eating Frenchmen dead,
And cut off Bonyparty's head? –
    And all that sort of thing.

So used I, when I was a boy,
To march with military toy,
    And ape the soldier's life;
And with a whistle or a hum,
I thought myself a Duke of Drum
    At least, or Earl of Fife.

With gun of tin and sword of lath,
Lord! how I walked in glory's path
    With regimental mates,
By sound of trump and rub-a-dubs –
To 'siege the wash-house – charge the tubs –
    Or storm the garden gates.

Ah me, my retrospective soul!
As over memory's muster-roll
    I cast my eyes anew,
My former comrades all the while
Rise up before me, rank and file,
    And form in dim review.

Ay, there they stand, and dress in line,
Lubbock, and Fenn, and David Vine,
    And dark "Jamaeky Forde"

And limping Wood, and "Cockey Hawes"
(Our captain always made, because
  He had a *real* sword!)

Thomas Hood (1799–1845)

Vitaï Lampada

There's a breathless hush in the Close tonight –
    Ten to make and the match to win –
A bumping pitch and a blinding light,
    An hour to play and the last man in.
And it's not for the sake of a ribboned coat,
    Or the selfish hope of a season's fame,
But his Captain's hand on his shoulder smote –
    "Play up! play up! and play the game!"

The sand of the desert is sodden red, –
    Red with the wreck of a square that broke; –
The Gatling's jammed and the Colonel dead,
    And the regiment blind with dust and smoke.
The river of death has brimmed his banks,
    And England's far, and Honour a name,
But the voice of a schoolboy rallies the ranks:
    "Play up! play up! and play the game!"

This is the word that year by year,
    While in her place the School is set,
Every one of her sons must hear,
    And none that hears it dare forget.
This they all with a joyful mind
    Bear through life like a torch in flame,
And falling fling to the host behind –
    "Play up! play up! and play the game!"

Sir Henry Newbolt (1899–1938)

from The Task

～

Great princes have great playthings. Some have
    played
At hewing mountains into men, and some
At building human wonders mountain-high.
Some have amused the dull, sad years of life
(Life spent in indolence, and therefore sad)
With schemes of monumental fame; and sought
By pyramids and mausolean pomp,
Short-lived themselves, t'immortalize their bones.
Some seek diversion in the tented field,
And make the sorrows of mankind their sport.
But war's a game which, were their subjects wise,
Kings would not play at. Nations would do well
T'extort their truncheons from the puny hands
Of heroes whose infirm and baby minds
Are gratified with mischief; and who spoil,
Because men suffer it, their toy the world.

              William Cowper (1731–1800)

The Drum

I hate that drum's discordant sound,
Parading round, and round, and round:
To thoughtless youth it pleasure yields,
And lures from cities and from fields,
To sell their liberty for charms
Of tawdry lace, and glittering arms;
And when Ambition's voice commands,
To march, and fight, and fall, in foreign lands.

I hate that drum's discordant sound,
Parading round, and round, and round:
To me it talks of ravaged plains,
And burning towns, and ruined swains,
And mangled limbs, and dying groans,
And widows' tears, and orphans' moans;
And all that Misery's hand bestows,
To fill the catalogue of human woes.

John Scott (1730–83)

Arthur McBride

I once knew a fellow named Arthur McBride,
And he and I rambled down by the seaside,
A-looking for pleasure or what might betide,
And the weather was pleasant and charming.

So gaily and gallant we went on our tramp,
And we met Sergeant Harper and Corporal Cramp,
And the little wee drummer who roused up the camp
With his row-de-dow-dow in the morning.

"Good morning, young fellow," the sergeant he cried,
"And the same to you, Sergeant," was all our reply.
There was nothing more spoken, we made to pass by,
And continue our walk in the morning.

"Well now, my fine fellows, if you will enlist,
A guinea in gold I will slap in your fist,
And a crown in the bargain to kick up the dust,
And drink the King's health in the morning."

"Oh no, Mister Sergeant, we aren't for sale,
We'll make no such bargain, and your bribe won't
    avail.

We're not tired of our country, and don't care to sail,
Though your offer is pleasant and charming.

"If we were such fools as to take your advance,
It's right bloody slender would be our poor chance,
For the King wouldn't scruple to send us to France
And get us all shot in the morning."

"How now, you young blackguards, if you say one
    more word,
I swear by the errins I'll draw out my sword
And run through your bodies as my strength may
    afford.
So now, you young buggers, take warning."

Well we beat that bold drummer as flat as a shoe,
And we made a football of his row-de-dow-dow,
And as for the others we knocked out the two,
Oh, we were the boys in that morning.

We took our old weapons that hung by our side
And flung them as far as we could in the tide.
"May the devil do with you," says Arthur McBride,
"For delaying our walk this fine morning."

Anon (c. 1800)

from William Wrench

~

When I was sent to serve my Queen
(Which service had my credit been)
A soldier's life I counted base
And held it always in disgrace.

An idle life was my delight,
For which I took myself to flight,
And from my Captain secret came,
Regarding neither fear nor shame.

For which, myself, with divers more
Unto the number of three score,
Were searched and sought for, far and near,
And many of us taken were.

Myself (the more unhappy I)
With others two, were judged to die,
To be a warning to all those
That will not fight 'gainst England's foes.

Indeed I must confess for truth
I have been still a desperate youth

And have for many a wilful crime
Deservéd death before this time.

Licentiously I spent my life,
And gave my mind to brawls and strife;
And he that could best drink and swill
I took for my companion still.

Let young men all that live at ease
Take heed by me how they displease
Their virtuous Prince, as I have done;
But, for her sake, no dangers shun.

If I had died in mother's womb,
Blessed had I been in such a tomb;
But I was born with shame to die,
(Break, heart!) the more unhappy I.

If in the wars I had been slain,
I should not then this shame sustain.
Then, gallant boys, make this your hope:
A bullet's better than a rope.

Anon (c. 1600)

from Jerusalem

Is not the wound of the sword sweet & the broken
    bone delightful?
Wilt thou now smile among the scythes when the
    wounded groan in the field?
We were carried away in thousands from London & in
    tens
Of thousands from Westminster & Marybone, in
    ships closed up,
Chained hand & foot, compelled to fight under the
    iron whips
Of our captains, fearing our officers more than the
    enemy.

William Blake (1757–1827)

from **Horestes**

~

Farewell, adieu, that courtlike life,
    To war we tend to go,
It is good sport to see the strife
    Of soldiers on a row.
        How merrily they forward march
        These enemies to slay,
        With hey, trim, and tricksy too,
        Their banners they display.

Now shall we have the golden cheats,
    When others want the same,
And soldiers have full many feats
    Their enemies to tame:
        With couching here, and booming there,
        They break their foes' array,
        And lusty ladies, amid the fields,
        Their ensigns do display.

The drum and flute play lustily.
   The trumpet blows amain,
And vent'rous knights courageously
   Do march before their train:
     With spear in rest so lively dressed,
     In armour bright and gay,
     With hey, trim and tricksy too,
     Their banners they display.

John Pickeryng (c. 1567)

The Soldier Going to the Field

Preserve thy sighs, unthrifty girl,
    To purify the air,
Thy tears to thread instead of pearl
    On bracelets of thy hair.

The trumpet makes the echo hoarse
    And wakes the louder drum;
Expense of grief gains no remorse
    When sorrow must be dumb.

For I must go where lazy Peace
    Will hide her drowsy head,
And, for the sport of kings, increase
    The number of the dead.

But first I'll chide thy cruel theft:
    Can I in war delight,
Who being of my heart bereft
    Can have no heart to fight?

Thou know'st the sacred Laws of old
    Ordained a thief should pay,
To quit him of his theft, sevenfold
    What he has stolen away.

Thy payment shall but double be;
    Oh, then with speed resign
My own seducéd heart to me,
    Accompanied with thine.
                    Sir William Davenant (1606–68)

My Bonny Mary

Go fetch to me a pint of wine,
    And fill it in a silver tassie,
That I may drink before I go
    A service to my bonny lassie:
The boat rocks at the pier of Leith,
    Full loud the wind blaws frae the ferry,
The ship rides by the Berwick-law,
    And I maun leave my bonny Mary.

The trumpets sound, the banners fly,
    The glittering spears are rankéd ready;
The shouts of war are heard afar,
    The battle closes thick and bloody;
But it's not the roar of sea or shore
    Wad make me langer wish to tarry;
Nor shouts of war that's heard afar –
    It's leaving thee, my bonny Mary.

Robert Burns (1759–96)

from **Henry IV, Part One**

～

HOTSPUR: I must leave you within these two hours.
KATE: Oh, my good lord, why are you thus alone?
    For what offence have I this fortnight been
    A banished woman from my Harry's bed?
    Tell me, sweet lord, what is't that takes from thee
    Thy stomach, pleasure, and thy golden sleep?
    Why dost thou bend thine eyes upon the earth,
    And start so often when thou sitt'st alone?
    Why hast thou lost the fresh blood in thy cheeks,
    And given my treasures and my rights of thee
    To thick-eyed musing and cursed melancholy?
    In thy faint slumbers I by thee have watched,
    And heard thee murmur tales of iron wars,
    Speak terms of manage to thy bounding steed,
    Cry, "Courage! To the field!" And thou hast talked
    Of sallies and retires, of trenches, tents,
    Of pallisadoes, frontiers, parapets,
    Of basilisks, of cannon, culverin,
    Of prisoners' ransom, and of soldiers slain,
    And all the currents of a heady fight.
              William Shakespeare (1564–1616)

Going to the Wars

Tell me not (sweet) I am unkind,
    That from the nunnery
Of thy chaste breast, and quiet mind,
    To war and arms I fly.

True: a new mistress now I chase,
    The first foe in the field;
And with a stronger faith embrace
    A sword, a horse, a shield.

Yet this inconstancy is such
    As you too shall adore;
I could not love thee (dear) so much,
    Loved I not Honour more.

Richard Lovelace (1618–58)

from The Volunteer

~

'Twas in that memorable year
France threatened to put off in
Flat-bottomed boats, intending each
To be a British coffin,
To make sad widows of our wives,
And every babe an orphan –

When coats were made of scarlet cloaks,
And heads were dredged with flour,
I 'listed in the Lawyers' Corps,
Against the battle hour;
A perfect Volunteer – for why?
I brought my "will and pow'r."

One dreary day – a day of dread,
Like Cato's, overcast –
About the hour of six (the morn
And I were breaking fast)
There came a loud and sudden sound,
That struck me all aghast.

*   *   *

The captain marched as mourners march,
The ensign too seemed lagging,
And many more, although they were
No ensigns, took to flagging –
Like corpses in the Serpentine,
Methought they wanted dragging.

But while I watched, the thought of death
Came like a chilly gust,
And lo! I shut the window down,
With very little lust
To join so many marching men,
That soon might be March dust.

Quoth I, "Since Fate ordains it so,
Our foe the coast must land on."
I felt so warm beside the fire
I cared not to abandon;
Our hearths and homes are always things
That patriots make a stand on.

"The fools that fight abroad for home,"
Thought I, "may get a wrong one;
Let those that have no home at all
Go battle for a long one."

The mirror here confirmed me this
Reflection, by a strong one.

For there, where I was wont to shave,
And deck me like Adonis,
There stood the leader of our foes,
With vultures for his cronies –
No Corsican but Death itself,
The Bony of all Bonies.

A horrid sight it was, and sad,
To see the grisly chap
Put on my crimson livery
And then begin to clap
My helmet on – ah me! It felt
Like any felon's cap.

My plume seemed borrowed from a hearse,
An undertaker's crest;
My epaulettes like coffin-plates;
My belt so heavy-pressed,
Four pipeclay cross-roads seemed to lie
At once upon my breast.

My brazen breastplate only lacked
A little heap of salt,
To make me like a corpse full dressed,
Preparing for the vault –
To set up what the Poet calls
My everlasting halt.

This funeral show inclined me quite
To peace; – and here I am!
Whilst better lions go to war,
Enjoying with the lamb
A lengthened life, that might have been
A martial epigram.

Thomas Hood (1799–1845)

Martial Elegy

How glorious fall the valiant, sword in hand,
In front of battle for their native land!
But, oh! What ills await the wretch that yields,
A recreant outcast from his country's fields!
The mother whom he loves shall quit her home,
An agéd father at his side shall roam,
His little ones shall weeping with him go,
And a young wife participate his woe;
While scorned and scowled upon by every face,
They pine for food, and beg from place to place.

Stain of his breed! Dishonouring manhood's form,
All ills shall cleave to him: – Affliction's storm
Shall bind him wandering in the vale of years,
Till, lost to all but ignominious fears,
He shall not blush to leave a recreant's name,
And children, like himself, inured to shame.

But we will combat for our fathers' land,
And we will drain the life-blood where we stand,
To save our children: – fight ye side by side,
And serried close, ye men of youthful pride,
Disdaining fear, and deeming light the cost
Of life itself in glorious battle lost.

Leave not our sires to stem the unequal fight,
Whose limbs are nerved no more with buoyant might;
Nor, lagging backward, let the younger breast
Permit the man of age (a sight unblessed)
To welter in the combat's foremost thrust,
His hoary head dishevelled in the dust,
And venerable bosom bleeding bare.

But youth's fair form, though fallen, is ever fair,
And beautiful in death the boy appears,
The hero boy, that dies in blooming years;
In man's regret he lives, and woman's tears,
More sacred than in life, and lovelier far,
For having perished in the front of war.

Tyrtaeus (c. 600 BC)
translated by Thomas Campbell (1777–1844)

Dulce et Decorum Est

~

Bent double, like old beggars under sacks,
Knock-kneed, coughing like hags, we cursed through
    sludge,
Till on the haunting flares we turned our backs,
And towards our distant rest began to trudge.
Men marched asleep; many had lost their boots,
But limped on, blood-shod. All went lame, all blind;
Drunk with fatigue; deaf even to the hoots
Of gas-shells dropping softly behind.

Gas! GAS! Quick, boys! – An ecstasy of fumbling
Fitting the clumsy helmets just in time,
But someone still was yelling out and stumbling,
And flound'ring like a man in fire or lime –
Dim through the misty panes and thick green light,
As under a green sea, I saw him drowning.

In all my dreams, before my helpless sight
He plunges at me, guttering, choking, drowning.

If in some smothering dreams you too could pace
Behind the wagon that we flung him in,
And watch the white eyes writhing in his face,
His hanging face, like a devil's sick of sin,
If you could hear, at every jolt, the blood
Come gargling from the froth-corrupted lungs,
Bitten as the cud
Of vile, incurable sores on innocent tongues, –
My friend, you would not tell with such high zest
To children ardent for some desperate glory,
The old Lie: *Dulce et decorum est*
Pro patria mori.

Wilfred Owen (1893–1918)

from Hamlet

~

HAMLET: Good sir, whose powers are these?

CAPTAIN: They are of Norway, sir.

HAMLET: How purposed, sir, I pray you?

CAPTAIN: Against some part of Poland.

HAMLET: Who commands them, sir?

CAPTAIN: The nephew to old Norway, Fortinbras.

HAMLET: Goes it against the main of Poland, sir,
Or for some frontier?

CAPTAIN: Truly to speak, and with no addition,
We go to gain a little patch of ground
That hath in it no profit but the name.
To pay five ducats – five – I would not farm it;
Nor will it yield to Norway or the Pole
A ranker rate should it be sold in fee.

HAMLET: Why, then the Polack never will defend it.

CAPTAIN: Yes, it is already garrisoned.

HAMLET: Two thousand souls and twenty thousand
ducats
Will not debate the question of this straw!
This is th'imposthume of much wealth and peace,
That inward breaks, and shows no cause without
Why the man dies.

William Shakespeare (1564–1616)

Ball's Bluff: A Reverie

~

One noonday, at my window in the town,
   I saw a sight – saddest that eyes can see –
   Young soldiers marching lustily
        Unto the wars,
With fifes, and flags in mottoed pageantry;
     While all the porches, walks, and doors
Were rich with ladies cheering royally.

They moved like Juny morning on the wave,
   Their hearts were fresh as clover in its prime
   (It was the breezy summer time),
       Life throbbed so strong,
How should they dream that Death in a rosy
       clime
     Would come to thin their shining throng?
Youth feels immortal, like the gods sublime.

Weeks passed; and at my window, leaving bed,
   By night I mused, of easeful sleep bereft,
   On those brave boys (Ah War! thy theft);
       Some marching feet

Found pause at last by cliffs Potomac cleft;
  Wakeful I mused, while in the street
Far footfalls died away till none were left.

Herman Melville (1819–91)

Chapter 2

WHO GOES THERE?

Night falls on the eve of battle: another point of no return. As "darkness crumbles away" into daylight, here is the calm before the storm, a time of hope and fear and of last-minute memories. Some of the poets in this section acutely hear, as if for the first time, the rustling of nature beneath the stars; others sense the spirits of those who have been here before, and invoke the ghosts of soldiers and of poets . . .

Bivouac on a Mountain Side

~

I see before me now a traveling army halting,
Below a fertile valley spread, with barns and the
    orchards of summer,
Behind, the terraced sides of a mountain, abrupt, in
    places rising high,
Broken, with rocks, with clinging cedars, with tall
    shapes dingily seen,
The numerous camp-fires scattered near and far,
    some away up on the mountain,
The shadowy forms of men and horses, looming,
    large-sized, flickering,
And over the sky – the sky! far, far out of reach,
    studded, breaking out, the eternal stars.

Walt Whitman (1819 – 92)

from Elegy Written in a Country Churchyard

The curfew tolls the knell of parting day,
The lowing herd wind slowly o'er the lea,
The plowman homeward plods his weary way,
And leaves the world to darkness and to me.

Now fades the glimmering landscape on the sight,
And all the air a solemn stillness holds,
Save where the beetle wheels his droning flight,
And drowsy tinklings lull the distant folds . . .

Beneath those rugged elms, that yew-tree's shade,
Where heaves the turf in many a mould'ring heap,
Each in his narrow cell for ever laid,
The rude forefathers of the hamlet sleep . . .

Full many a gem of purest ray serene,
The dark unfathomed caves of ocean bear:
Full many a flower is born to blush unseen,
And waste its sweetness on the desert air.

Thomas Gray (1716–71)

A Dweller in Wipers' Elegy to that Town

A six-inch tolls the knell of parting day.
The transport cart winds slowly o'er the lea.
A sapper homeward plods his weary way,
And leaves the world to Wipers and to me.

Now fades the glimmering star shell from the sight,
And all the air a solemn stillness holds;
Save where a whizzbang howls its rapid flight
And "five-rounds-rapid" fill the distant folds.

Beneath the ramparts old and grim and grey,
In earthy sap, and casement cool and deep;
Each in his canvas cubicle and bay,
The men condemned to Wipers soundly sleep.

Full many a man will venture out by day,
Deceived by what he thinks a quiet spell;
Till to a crump he nearly falls a prey
And into neighbouring cellar bolts like hell.

A burning mountain belching forth its fire,
A sandstorm in the desert in full fling;
Or Hades with its lid prised off entire,
Is naught to dear old Wipers in the Spring.

Anon (1916)

Into Battle

The naked earth is warm with Spring,
And with green grass and bursting trees
Leans to the sun's gaze glorying,
And quivers in the sunny breeze;
And life is Colour and Warmth and Light,
And a striving evermore for these;
And he is dead who will not fight;
And who dies fighting has increase.

The fighting man shall from the sun
Take warmth, and life from the glowing earth;
Speed with the light-foot winds to run,
And with the trees to newer birth;
And find, when fighting shall be done,
Great rest, and fullness after dearth.

All the bright company of Heaven
Hold him in their high comradeship,
The Dog-Star, and the Sisters Seven,
Orion's Belt and sworded hip.

The woodland trees that stand together,
They stand to him each one a friend,
They gently speak in the windy weather;
They guide to valley and ridge's end.

The kestrel hovering by day,
And the little owls that call by night,
Bid him be swift and keen as they,
As keen of ear, as swift of sight.

The blackbird sings to him, "Brother, brother,
If this be the last song you shall sing,
Sing well, for you may not sing another;
    Brother, sing."

In dreary, doubtful, waiting hours,
Before the brazen frenzy starts,
The horses show him nobler powers;
O patient eyes, courageous hearts!

And when the burning moment breaks,
And all things else are out of mind,
And only Joy of Battle takes
Him by the throat, and makes him blind.

Through joy and blindness he shall know,
Not caring much to know, that still
Nor lead nor steel shall reach him, so
That it be not the Destined Will.

The thundering line of battle stands,
And in the air Death moans and sings;
But Day shall clasp him with strong hands,
And Night shall fold him in soft wings.

Julian Grenfell (1888–1915)

The French and the Spanish Guerrillas

~

Hunger, and sultry heat, and nipping blast
From bleak hilltop, and length of march by night
Through heavy swamp, or over snow-clad height,
These hardships ill sustained, these dangers past,
The roving Spanish bands are reached at last,
Charged, and dispersed like foam: – but as a flight
Of scattered quails by signs do reunite,
So these, – and, heard of once again, are chased
With combinations of long-practised art
And newly kindled hope; but they are fled,
Gone are they, viewless as the buried dead;
Where now? – Their sword is at the foeman's heart!
And thus from year to year his walk they thwart,
And hang like dreams around his guilty bed.

William Wordsworth (1770–1850)

from Richard III

~

Enter the Ghost of Buckingham
GHOST: The first was I that helped thee to the crown;
The last was I that felt thy tyranny.
O, in the battle think of Buckingham,
And die in terror of thy guiltiness.
Dream on, dream on of bloody deeds and death;
Fainting, despair: despairing, yield thy breath.
Richard starteth up out of a dream
RICHARD: Give me another horse! Bind up my
wounds!
Have mercy, Jesu! – Soft – I did but dream.
O coward conscience, how dost thou afflict me!
The lights burn blue; it is now dead midnight.
Cold fearful drops stand on my trembling flesh.
What do I fear? Myself? There's none else by;
Richard loves Richard, that is, I and I.
Is there a murderer here? No. Yes, I am!
Then fly. What, from myself? Great reason why,
Lest I revenge? What, myself upon myself?
William Shakespeare (1564–1616)

The Soldier's Dream

Our bugles sang truce, for the night-cloud had
    lowered,
And the sentinel stars set their watch in the sky;
And thousands had sunk on the ground overpowered,
The weary to sleep and the wounded to die.

When reposing that night on my pallet of straw,
By the wolf-scaring faggot that guarded the slain,
At the dead of the night a sweet vision I saw,
And thrice ere the morning I dreamt it again.

Methought from the battlefield's dreadful array,
Far, far I had roamed on a desolate track:
'Twas Autumn, – and sunshine arose on the way
To the home of my fathers, that welcomed me back.

I flew to the pleasant fields traversed so oft
In life's morning march, when my bosom was young;
I heard my own mountain-goats bleating aloft,
And knew the sweet strain that the corn-reapers
    sung.

Then pledged we the wine-cup, and fondly I swore,
From my home and my weeping friends never to part.
My little ones kissed me a thousand times o'er,
And my wife sobbed aloud in her fullness of heart.

Stay, stay with us, – rest, thou art weary and worn!
And fain was their war-broken soldier to stay; –
But sorrow returned with the dawning of morn,
And the voice in my dreaming ear melted away.

Thomas Campbell (1777–1844)

Soldier's Dream

I dreamed kind Jesus fouled the big-gun gears;
And caused a permanent stoppage in all bolts;
And buckled with a smile Mausers and Colts;
And rusted every bayonet with His tears.

And there were no more bombs, of ours or Theirs,
Not even an old flint-lock, nor even a pikel.
But God was vexed, and gave power to Michael;
And when I woke he'd seen to our repairs.

Wilfred Owen (1893–1918)

A New Year's Eve in War Time

Phantasmal fears,
And the flap of the flame,
And the throb of the clock,
And a loosened slate,
And the blind night's drone,
Which tiredly the spectral pines intone.

And the blood in my ears
Strumming always the same,
And the gable-cock
With its fitful grate,
And myself, alone.

The twelfth hour nears
Hand-hid, as in shame;
I undo the lock,
And listen and wait
For the Young Unknown.

In the dark there careers –
As if Death astride came
To numb all with his knock –

A horse at mad rate
Over rut and stone.

No figure appears,
No call of my name,
No sound but "Tic-toc"
Without check. Past the gate
It clatters – is gone.

What rider it bears
There is none to proclaim;
And the Old Year has struck,
And scarce animate,
The New makes moan.

Maybe that "More Tears! –
More Famine and Flame –
More Severance and Shock!"
Is the order from Fate
That the Rider speeds on
To pale Europe; and tiredly the pines intone.

Thomas Hardy (1840–1928)

from Polyolbion

In that black night before his sad and dismal day
Were apparitions strange – as dread Heaven would
    bewray
The horrors to ensue. Oh, most amazing sight!
Two armies in the air discernéd were to fight,
Which came so near to earth that in the morn they
    found
The prints of horses' feet remaining in the ground,
Which came but as a show, the time to entertain
Till th'angry armies joined to act the bloody scene.
Shrill shouts, and deadly cries, each way the air do
    fill,
And not a word was heard from either side, but "Kill!"
The father 'gainst the son, the brother 'gainst the
    brother,
With glaives, swords, bills, and pikes, were murdering
    one another.
The full luxurious earth seems surfeited with blood
Whilst in his uncle's gore th' unnatural nephew stood.

Whilst with their charged staves, the desperate
  horsemen meet,
They hear their kinsmen groan under their horses'
  feet.
Dead men and weapons broke do on the earth
  abound;
The drums bedashed with brains, do give a dismal
  sound.

Michael Drayton (1563–1631)

from The Seasons: Autumn

Oft in this season, silent from the north
A blaze of meteors shoots – ensweeping first
The lower skies, they all at once converge
High to the crown of heaven, and, all at once
Relapsing quick, as quickly re-ascend,
And mix and thwart, extinguish and renew,
All ether coursing in a maze of light.
⠀⠀⠀From look to look, contagious through the crowd,
The panic runs, and into wondrous shapes
The appearance throws – armies in meet array,
Thronged with aerial spears and steeds of fire;
Till, the long lines of full-extended war
In bleeding fight commixed, the sanguine flood
Rolls a broad slaughter o'er the plains of heaven.
As thus they scan the visionary scene,
On all sides swells the superstitious din,
Incontinent; and busy frenzy talks
Of blood and battle; cities overturned,
And late at night in swallowing earthquake sunk,
Or hideous wrapped in fierce ascending flame;
Of sallow famine, inundation, storm;
Of pestilence, and every great distress;

Empires subversed, when ruling fate has struck
The unalterable hour: even Nature's self
Is deemed to totter on the brink of time.

James Thomson (1700–48)

The Night Before Agincourt *from* Henry V

~

Now entertain conjecture of a time
When creeping murmur and the poring dark
Fills the wide vessel of the universe.
From camp to camp through the foul womb of night
The hum of either army stilly sounds,
That the fixed sentinels almost receive
The secret whispers of each other's watch.
Fire answers fire, and through their paly flames
Each battle sees the other's umbered face.
Steed threatens steed in high and boastful neighs,
Piercing the night's dull ear. And from the tents
The armourers, accomplishing the knights,
With busy hammers closing rivets up,
Give dreadful note of preparation.
The country cocks do crow, the clocks do toll,
And the third hour of drowsy morning name.
Proud of their numbers and secure in soul,
The confident and over-lusty French
Do the low-rated English play at dice,
And chide the cripple tardy-gaited Night
Who like a foul and ugly witch doth limp
So tediously away. The poor condemnéd English,

Like sacrifices, by their watchful fires
Sit patiently and inly ruminate
The morning's danger; and their gesture sad,
Investing lank-lean cheeks and war-torn coats
Presenteth them unto the gazing moon
So many horrid ghosts.

William Shakespeare (1564–1616)

I Have a Rendezvous with Death . . .

～

I have a rendezvous with Death
At some disputed barricade,
When Spring comes back with rustling shade
And apple-blossoms fill the air –
I have a rendezvous with Death
When Spring brings back blue days and fair.

It may be he shall take my hand
And lead me into his dark land
And close my eyes and quench my breath –
It may be I shall pass him still.
I have a rendezvous with Death
On some scarred slope of battered hill,
When Spring comes round again this year
And the first meadow-flowers appear.

God knows 'twere better to be deep
Pillowed in silk and scented down,
Where love throbs out in blissful sleep,
Pulse nigh to pulse, and breath to breath,
Where hushed awakenings are dear . . .

But I've a rendezvous with Death
At midnight in some flaming town
When Spring trips north again this year,
And I to my pledged word am true,
I shall not fail that rendezvous.

Alan Seeger (1888–1916)

The Night Before an Engagement
(Written at Sea in the First Dutch War, 1665)

To all you ladies now at land
    We men at sea indite;
But first would have you understand
    How hard it is to write.
The Muses now, and Neptune too,
We must implore to write to you,

For tho' the Muses should prove kind,
    And fill our empty brain;
Yet if rough Neptune rouse the wind,
    To wave the azure main,
Our paper, pen, and ink, and we,
Roll up and down our ships at sea.

Then, if we write not by each post,
    Think not we are unkind;
Nor yet conclude our ships are lost
    By Dutchmen, or by wind:
Our tears we'll send a speedier way,
The tide shall bring 'em twice a day.

The king with wonder, and surprise,
　　Will swear the seas grow bold;
Because the tides will higher rise,
　　Than e'er they used of old:
But let him know it is our tears
Bring floods of grief to Whitehall stairs.

Should foggy Opdam chance to know
　　Our sad and dismal story;
The Dutch would scorn so weak a foe,
　　And quit their fort at Goree:
For what resistance can they find
From men who've left their hearts behind!

Let wind and weather do its worst,
　　Be you to us but kind;
Let Dutchmen vapour, Spaniards curse,
　　No sorrow we shall find:
'Tis then no matter how things go,
Or who's our friend, or who's our foe.

To pass the tedious hours away,
　　We throw a merry main;
Or else at serious ombre play;
　　But, why would we in vain

Each others' ruin thus pursue?
We were undone when we left you.

But now our fears tempestuous grow,
      And cast our hopes away;
Whilst you, regardless of our woe,
      Sit careless at a play:
Perhaps permit some happier man
To kiss your hand, or flirt your fan.

When any mournful tune you hear,
      That dies in ev'ry note;
As if it sighed with each man's care,
      For being so remote;
Think then how often love we've made
To you when all those tunes were played.

In justice you cannot refuse,
      To think of our distress;
When we for hopes of honour lose
      Our certain happiness;
All those designs are but to prove
Ourselves more worthy of your love.

And now we've told you all our loves,
  And likewise all our fears;
In hopes this declaration moves
  Some pity from your tears:
Let's hear of no inconstancy,
We have too much of that at sea.

Charles Sackville, Earl of Dorset
(1638–1706)

Love's War

Till I have peace with thee, war other men,
And when I have peace, can I leave thee then?
All other wars are scrupulous; only thou,
O fair free city, maist thyself allow
To any one. In Flanders, who can tell
Whether the master press; or men rebel?
Only we know, that which all idiots say,
They bear most blows which come to part the fray.
France in her lunatic giddiness did hate
Ever our men, yea and our God of late;
Yet she relies upon our angels well,
Which ne'er return; no more than they which fell.
Sick Ireland is with a strange war possessed
Like to an ague; now raging, now at rest;
Which time will cure: yet it must do her good
If she were purged, and her head vain let blood.
And Midas joys our Spanish journeys give,
We touch all gold, but find no food to live.
And I should be in the hot parching clime
To dust and ashes turned before my time
To mew me in a ship is to enthral
Me in a prison, that were like to fall;

Or in a cloister; save that there men dwell
In a calm heaven, here in swaggering hell.
Long voyages are long consumptions,
And ships are carts for executions
Yea they are deaths. Is't not all one to fly
Into another world, as 'tis to die?
Here let me war; in these arms let me lie;
Here let me parley, batter, bleed and die.
Thine arms imprison me, and mine arms thee;
Thy heart thy ransom is; take mine for me.
Other men war that they their rest may gain;
But we will rest that we may fight again.
Those wars the ignorant, these th'experienced love,
There we are always under, here above.
There engines far off breed a just true fear,
Ne'er thrusts, pikes, stabs, yea, bullets hurt not here.
There lies are wrongs; here safe uprightly lie;
There men kill men, we will make one by and by.
Thou nothing; I not half so much shall do
In these wars, as they may which from us two
Shall spring. Thousands we see which travel not
To wars; But stay swords, arms, and shot,
To make at home; And shall not I do then
More glorious service, staying to make men?

John Donne (1573–1631)

The Soldier

Home furthest off grows dearer from the way;
And when the army in the Indias lay
Friends' letters coming from his native place
Were like old neighbours with their country face.
And every opportunity that came
Opened the sheet to gaze upon the name
Of that loved village where he left his sheep
For more contented peaceful folk to keep;
And friendly faces absent many a year
Would from such letters in his mind appear.
And when his pockets, chafing through the case,
Wore it quite out ere others took the place,
Right loath to be of company bereft
He kept the fragments while a bit was left.

John Clare (1793–1864)

The Soldier

~

If I should die, think only this of me:
　　That there's some corner of a foreign field
That is for ever England. There shall be
　　In that rich earth a richer dust concealed;
A dust whom England bore, shaped, made aware,
　　Gave, once, her flowers to love, her ways to roam,
A body of England's, breathing English air,
　　Washed by the rivers, blessed by suns of home.

And think, this heart, all evil shed away,
　　A pulse in the eternal mind, no less
　　　　Gives somewhere back the thoughts by
　　　　　　England given;
Her sights and sounds; dreams happy as her day;
　　And laughter, learnt of friends; and gentleness,
　　　　In hearts of peace, under an English heaven.
Rupert Brooke (1887–1915)

The Eve of Waterloo

The eyelids of eve fall together at last,
And the forms so foreign to field and tree
Lie down as though native, and slumber fast!

Sore are the thrills of misgiving we see
In the artless champaign at this harlequinade,
Distracting a vigil where calm should be!

The green seems opprest, and the plain afraid
Of a Something to come, whereof these are the
    proofs, –
Neither earthquake, nor storm, nor eclipse's shade!

Yea, the coneys are scared by the thud of hoofs,
And their white scuts flash at their vanishing heels,
And swallows abandon the hamlet-roofs.

The mole's tunnelled chambers are crushed by
    wheels,
The lark's eggs scattered, their owners fled;
And the hedgehog's household the sapper unseals.

The snail draws in at the terrible tread,
But in vain; he is crushed by the felloe-rim;
The worm asks what can be overhead,

And wriggles deep from a scene so grim,
And guesses him safe; for he does not know
What a foul red flood will be soaking him!

Beaten about by the heel and toe
Are the butterflies, sick of the day's long rheum,
To die of a worse than the weather-foe.

Trodden and bruised to a miry tomb
Are ears that have greened but will never be gold,
And flowers in the bud that will never bloom.

So the season's intent, ere its fruit unfold,
Is frustrate, and mangled, and made succumb,
Like a youth of promise struck stark and cold! . . .

And what of these who tonight have come?
The young sleep sound; but the weather awakes
In the veterans, pain from the past that numb;

Old stabs of Ind, old Peninsular aches,
Old Friedland chills, haunt their moist mud bed,
Cramps from Austerlitz; till their slumber breaks.

And each soul shivers as he sinks his head
On the loam he's to lease with the other dead
From tomorrow's mist-fall till Time be sped!
Thomas Hardy (1840–1928)

Break of Day in the Trenches

The darkness crumbles away –
It is the same old druid Time as ever.
Only a live thing leaps my hand –
A queer sardonic rat –
As I pull the parapet's poppy
To stick behind my ear.
Droll rat, they would shoot you if they knew
Your cosmopolitan sympathies
(And God knows what antipathies).
Now you have touched this English hand
You will do the same to a German –
Soon, no doubt, if it be your pleasure
To cross the sleeping green between.
It seems you inwardly grin as you pass
Strong eyes, fine limbs, haughty athletes
Less chanced than you for life,
Bonds to the whims of murder,
Sprawled in the bowels of the earth,
The torn fields of France.
What do you see in our eyes
At the shrieking iron and flame
Hurled through still heavens?

What quaver – what heart aghast?
Poppies whose roots are in man's veins
Drop, and are ever dropping;
But mine in my ear is safe,
Just a little white with the dust.

Isaac Rosenberg (1890–1918)

from Childe Harold's Pilgrimage

~

There was a sound of revelry by night,
    And Belgium's capital had gathered then
    Her beauty and her chivalry – and bright
    The lamps shone o'er fair women and brave men;
    A thousand hearts beat happily; and when
    Music arose with its voluptuous swell,
    Soft eyes looked love to eyes which spake again,
    And all went merry as a marriage-bell;
But hush! hark! a deep sound strikes like a rising
    knell!

Did ye not hear it? – No – 'twas but the wind,
    Or the car rattling o'er the stony street;
    On with the dance! let joy be unconfined;
    No sleep till morn, when youth and pleasure meet
    To chase the glowing hours with flying feet –
    But hark! – that heavy sound breaks in once more,
    As if the clouds its echo would repeat;
    And nearer – clearer – deadlier than before!
Arm! Arm! it is – it is – the cannon's opening roar!
       George Gordon, Lord Byron (1788–1824)

Chapter 3

CHARGE!

And after the calm, the storm: "On came the whirlwind!"
From Troy to No Man's Land, poets have looked to the
natural elements in seeking to measure the violence of war,
a force which (in the words of the Elizabethan poet
Nicholas Breton) "thunders in the air, rips up the earth,
cuts through the seas, and consumes with the fire" . . .

The Charge of the Light Brigade

~

Half a league, half a league,
　　Half a league onward,
All in the valley of Death
　　Rode the six hundred.
"Forward, the Light Brigade!
Charge the guns!" he said:
Into the valley of Death
　　Rode the six hundred.

"Forward the Light Brigade!"
Was there a man dismayed?
Not though the soldier knew
　　Someone had blundered:
Their's not to make reply,
Their's not to reason why,
Their's but to do or die:
Into the valley of Death
　　Rode the six hundred.

Cannon to right of them,
Cannon to left of them,
Cannon in front of them

Volleyed and thundered;
Stormed at with shot and shell,
Boldly they rode and well,
Into the jaws of Death
Into the mouth of Hell
    Rode the six hundred.

Flashed all their sabres bare,
Flashed as they turned in air
Sabring the gunners there,
Charging an army, while
    All the world wondered:
Plunged in the battery smoke
Right through the line they broke;
Cossack and Russian
Reeled from the sabre-stroke
    Shattered and sundered.
Then they rode back, but not
    Not the six hundred.

Cannon to right of them,
Cannon to left of them,
Cannon behind them
    Volleyed and thundered;

Stormed at with shot and shell,
While horse and hero fell,
They that had fought so well
Came through the jaws of Death,
Back from the mouth of Hell,
All that was left of them,
    Left of six hundred.

When can their glory fade?
O the wild charge they made!
    All the world wondered.
Honour the charge they made!
Honour the Light Brigade,
    Noble six hundred!
        Alfred Lord Tennyson (1809–92)

from Henry V

～

Once more unto the breach, dear friends, once more,
Or close the wall up with our English dead.
In peace there's nothing so becomes a man
As modest stillness and humility;
But when the blast of war blows in our ears,
Then imitate the action of the tiger:
Stiffen the sinews, conjure up the blood,
Disguise fair nature with hard-favoured rage.
Then lend the eye a terrible aspect;
Let it pry thorough the portage of the head
Like the brass cannon; let the brow o'erwhelm it
As fearfully as doth a galled rock
O'erhang and jutty his confounded base,
Swilled with the wild and wasteful ocean.
Now set the teeth and stretch the nostril wide,
Hold hard the breath and bend up every spirit
To his full height. On, on, you noble English,
Whose blood is fet from fathers of war-proof,
Fathers that like so many Alexanders
Have in these parts from morn till even fought,
And sheathed their swords for lack of argument.
Dishonour not your mothers; now attest

That those whom you called fathers did beget you.
Be copy now to men of grosser blood
And teach them how to war. And you, good yeomen,
Whose limbs were made in England, show us here
The mettle of your pasture: let us swear
That you are worth your breeding – which I doubt
   not,
For there is none of you so mean and base
That hath not noble lustre in your eyes.
I see you stand like greyhounds in the slips,
Straining upon the start. The game's afoot.
Follow your spirit, and upon this charge
Cry "God for Harry, England and Saint George!"

                   William Shakespeare (1564–1616)

from The Campaign

~

Behold in awful march and dread array
The long-extended squadrons shape their way!
Death, in approaching terrible, imparts
An anxious horror to the bravest hearts;
Yet do their beating breasts demand the strife,
And thirst of glory quells the love of life.
No vulgar fears can British minds control:
Heat of revenge, and noble pride of soul
O'erlook the foe, advantaged by his past,
Lessen his numbers, and contract his host.
Tho' fens and floods possessed the middle space,
That unprovoked they would have feared to pass;
Nor fens nor floods can stop Britannia's bands,
When her proud foe ranged on their borders stands.
  But O, my muse, what numbers wilt thou find
To sing the furious troops in battle joined!
Methinks I hear the drum's tumultuous sound
The victor's shouts and dying groans confound,
The dreadful burst of cannon rend the skies,
And all the thunder of the battle rise.
'Twas then Great Marlboro's mighty soul was proved
That, in the shock of charging hosts unmoved,

Amidst confusion, horror and despair,
Examined all the dreadful scenes of war;
In peaceful thought the field of death surveyed,
To fainting squadrons sent the timely aid
Inspired repulsed battalions to engage,
And taught the doubtful battle where to rage.
So when an angel by divine command
With rising tempests shakes a guilty land
Such as of late o'er pale Britannia past,
Calm and serene he drives the furious blast;
And pleased th' Almighty's orders to perform,
Rides in the whirlwind, and directs the storm.

Joseph Addison (1672–1719)

from The Field of Waterloo

On came the whirlwind – like the last
But fiercest sweep of tempest-blast –
On came the whirlwind – steel-gleams broke
Like lightning through the rolling smoke;
    The war was waked anew,
Three hundred cannon-mouths roared loud,
And from their throats, with flash and cloud,
    Their showers of iron threw.
Beneath their fire, in full career,
Rushed on the ponderous cuirassier,
The lancer couched his ruthless spear,
And hurrying as to havoc near,
    The cohorts' eagles flew.
In one dark torrent, broad and strong,
The advancing onset rolled along,
Forth harbingered by fierce acclaim,
That, from the shroud of smoke and flame,
Pealed wildly the imperial name.

But on the British heart were lost
The terrors of the charging host;
For not an eye the storm that viewed

Changed its proud glance of fortitude,
Nor was one forward footstep stopped,
Though close beside a comrade dropped.
Fast as their ranks the thunders tear,
Fast they renewed each serried square;
And on the wounded and the slain
Closed their diminished files again,
Till from their line scarce spears' lengths three,
Emerging from the smoke they see
Helmet and plume, and panoply, –
　　　Then waked their fire at once!
Each musketeer's revolving knell
As fast, as regularly fell,
As when they practise to display
Their discipline on festal day.
　　　Then down went helm and lance,
Down were the eagle banners sent,
Down reeling steeds and riders went,
Corslets were pierced, and pennons rent;
　　　And to augment the fray,
Wheeled full against their staggering flanks,
The English horsemen's foaming ranks
　　　Forced their resistless way.
Then to the musket-knell succeeds
The clash of swords – the neigh of steeds –

As plies the smith his clanging trade,
Against the cuirass rang the blade;
And while amid their close array
The well-served cannon rent their way,
And while amid their scattered band
Raged the fierce rider's bloody brand,
Recoiled in common rout and fear,
Lancer and guard and cuirassier,
Horsemen and foot, – a mingled host,
Their leaders fall'n, their standards lost.

Sir Walter Scott (1771–1832)

from A Funeral Poem upon the Death
of Sir Francis Vere

~

    Nor was his judgement only so mature
In purposes, whose distance could endure
Deliberate advice; but did express
Itself as fully ripe with readiness
And order where the cause would not admit
The action any time to study it.
    And had so present a conceit (that did
Attend occasion as it offered)
That when the thunder of a hot alarm
Hath called him suddenly from sleep to arm,
Upon the instant of his waking, he
Did with such life and quick dexterity,
His troops direct, the service execute,
As practised printers set and distribute
Their letters – and more perfectly effected,
For what he did was not to be corrected!

                Cyril Tourneur (c. 1575–1627)

Incident of the French Camp

You know, we French stormed Ratisbon:
    A mile or so away,
On a little mound, Napoleon
    Stood on our storming-day;
With neck out-thrust, you fancy how,
    Legs wide, arms locked behind,
As if to balance the prone brow
    Oppressive of his mind.

Just as perhaps he mused "My plans
    That soar, to earth may fall,
Let once my army-leader Lannes
    Waver at yonder wall," —
Out 'twixt the battery-smokes there flew
    A rider, bound on bound
Full-galloping; nor bridle drew
    Until he reached the mound.

Then off there flung in smiling joy,
    And held himself erect
By just his horse's mane, a boy:
    You hardly could suspect —

(So tight he kept his lips compressed,
    Scarce any blood came through)
You looked twice ere you saw his breast
    Was all but shot in two.

"Well," cried he, "Emperor, by God's grace
    We've got you Ratisbon!
The Marshal's in the market-place,
    And you'll be there anon
To see your flag-bird flap his vans
    Where I, to heart's desire,
Perched him!" The chief's eye flashed; his plans
    Soared up again like fire.

The chief's eye flashed; but presently
    Softened itself, as sheathes
A film the mother-eagle's eye
    When her bruised eaglet breathes;
"You're wounded!" "Nay," the soldier's pride
    Touched to the quick, he said:
"I'm killed, Sire!" And, his chief beside,
    Smiling the boy fell dead.

Robert Browning (1812–89)

I Saw Old General at Bay

I saw old General at bay,
(Old as he was, his gray eyes yet shone out in battle
    like stars),
His small force was now completely hemmed in, in
    his works,
He called for volunteers to run the enemy's lines, a
    desperate emergency,
I saw a hundred and more step forth from the ranks,
    but two or three were selected,
I saw them receive the orders aside, they listened with
    care, the adjutant was very grave,
I saw them depart with cheerfulness, freely risking
    their lives.

Walt Whitman (1819–92)

from The Recruiting Serjeant

What a charming thing's a battle!
Trumpets sounding, drums a-beating;
Crack, crick, crack, the cannons rattle,
Ev'ry heart with joy elating.
With what pleasure are we spying,
From the front and from the rear,
Round us in the smoky air,
Heads and limbs and bullets flying!
Then the groans of soldiers dying,
Just like sparrows as it were:
At each pop,
Hundreds drop,
While the muskets prittle prattle.
Killed and wounded
Lie confounded:
What a charming thing's a battle!
But the pleasant joke of all
Is when to close attack we fall,
Like mad bulls each other butting,
Shooting, stabbing, maiming, cutting;
Horse and foot
All go to't,

Kill's the word, both men and cattle,
Then to plunder:
Blood and thunder,
What a charming thing's a battle!

Isaac Bickerstaffe (1733–?1812)

The Night Patrol

Over the top! The wire's thin here, unbarbed
Plain rusty coils, not staked, and low enough:
Full of old tins, though – "When you're through, all
    three,
Aim quarter left for fifty yards or so,
Then straight for that new piece of German wire;
See if it's thick, and listen for a while
For sounds of working; don't run any risks;
About an hour; now over!" And we placed
Our hands on the topmost sand-bags, leapt, and
    stood
A second with curved backs, then crept to the wire,
Wormed ourselves tinkling through, glanced back,
    and dropped.
The sodden ground was splashed with shallow pools,
And tufts of crackling cornstalks, two years old,
No man had reaped, and patches of spring grass,
Half-seen, as rose and sank the flares, were strewn
With the wrecks of our attack: the bandoliers,
Packs, rifles, bayonets, belts, and haversacks,
Shell fragments, and the huge whole forms of shells
Shot fruitlessly – and everywhere the dead.

Only the dead were always present – present
As a vile sickly smell of rottenness;
The rustling stubble and the early grass,
The slimy pools – the dead men stank through all,
Pungent and sharp; as bodies loomed before,
And as we passed, they stank; then dulled away
To that vague foetor, all encompassing,
Infecting earth and air. They lay, all clothed,
Each in some new and piteous attitude
That we well marked to guide us back; as he,
Outside our wire, that lay on his back and crossed
His legs Crusader-wise; I smiled at that,
And thought of Elia and his Temple Church.
From him, a quarter left, lay a small corpse,
Down in a hollow, huddled as in bed,
That one of us put his hand on unawares.
Next was a bunch of half a dozen men
All blown to bits, an archipelago
Of corrupt fragments, vexing to us three,
Who had no light to see by, save the flares.
On such a trail, so lit, for ninety yards
We crawled on belly and elbows, till we saw,
Instead of lumpish dead before our eyes,
The stakes and crosslines of the German wire.
We lay in shelter of the last dead man,

Ourselves as dead, and heard their shovels ring
Turning the earth, their talk and cough at times.
A sentry fired and a machine-gun spat;
They shot a flare above us, when it fell
And spluttered out in the pools of No Man's Land,
We turned and crawled past the remembered dead:
Past him and him, and them and him, until,
For he lay some way apart, we caught the scent
Of the Crusader and slid past his legs,
And through the wire and home, and got our rum.

Arthur Graeme West (1891–1917)

The Battle of Crécy
from The Reign of Edward III

~

For there, my lord, oh, there we did descry
Down in a valley how both armies lay.
The French had cast their trenches like a ring,
And every barricado's open front
Was thick-embossed with brazen ordinance;
Here stood a battle of ten thousand horse,
There twice as many pikes in quadrant wise,
Here crossbows, and deadly wounding darts:
And in the midst, like to a slender point
Within the compass of the horizon,
As 'twere a rising bubble in the sea,
A hazelwand amid a wood of pines,
Or as a bear fast-chained unto a stake,
Stood famous Edward, still expecting when
Those dogs of France would fasten on his flesh.
Anon the death-procuring knell begins:
Off go the cannons, that with trembling noise
Did shake the very mountain where they stood;
Then sound the trumpets' clangour in the air,
The battles join: and, when we could no more
Discern the difference 'twixt the friend and foe,

So intricate the dark confusion was,
Away we turned our wat'ry eyes with sighs,
As black as powder fuming into smoke.

Anon (c. 1590)

from Blenheim, A Poem

〜

Now from each van
The brazen instruments of death discharge
Horrible flames, and turbid streaming clouds
Of smoke sulphureous; intermixed with these
Large globous irons fly, of dreadful hiss,
Singeing the air, and from long distance bring
Surprising slaughter; on each side they fly
By chains connexed, and with destructive sweep
Behead whole troops at once; the hairy scalps
Are whirled aloof, while numerous trunks bestrow
Th' ensanguined field; with latent mischief stored
Show'rs of grenadoes rain, by sudden burst
Disploding murd'rous bowels, fragments of steel,
And stones, and glass, and nitrous grain adust.
A thousand ways at once the shivered orbs
Fly diverse, working torment and foul rout
With deadly bruise, and gashes furrowed deep.
Of pain impatient, the high-prancing steeds
Disdain the curb, and, flinging to and fro,
Spurn their dismounted riders; they expire
Indignant, by unhostile wounds destroyed.

Thus through each army Death in various shapes
Prevailed; here mangled limbs, here brains and gore
Lie clotted; lifeless some: with anguish these
Gnashing, and loud laments invoking aid,
Unpitied and unheard; the louder din
Of guns, and trumpets' clang, and solemn sound
Of drums, o'ercame their groans. In equal scale
Long hung the fight, few marks of fear were seen,
None of retreat. As when two adverse winds,
Sublimed from dewy vapours, in mid-sky
Engage with horrid shock, the ruffled brine
Roars stormy, they together dash the clouds,
Levying their equal force with utmost rage;
Long undecided lasts the airy strife.

John Philips (1676–1709)

from The Episode of Sarpedon

As when two scales are charged with doubtful loads,
From side to side the trembling balance nods,
Till poized aloft, the resting beam suspends
Each equal weight, nor this, nor that descends;
So conquest, loth for either to declare,
Levels her wings, and hov'ring hangs in air.
Till Hector came, to whose superior might
Jove owed the glory of the destined fight.
Fierce as a whirlwind, up the walls he flies,
And fires his host with loud repeated cries:
"Advance ye Trojans, lend your valiant hands,
Haste to the fleet, and toss the blazing brands!"
They hear, they run, and gath'ring at his call,
Raise scaling engines, and ascend the wall:
Around the works a wood of glitt'ring spears
Shoots up, and all the rising host appears.
A pondrous stone bold Hector heaved to throw,
Pointed above, and rough and gross below:
Not two strong men th'enormous weight could raise
(Such men as live in these degen'rate days)
Yet this, as easy as a swain would bear
The snowy fleece; he tossed, and shook in air:

For Jove upheld, and lightened of its load
Th'unwieldy rock, the labour of a god.
Thus armed, before the folded gates he came,
Of massy substance and stupendous frame,
With iron bars and brazen hinges strong,
On lofty beams of solid timber hung.
Then thund'ring thro' the planks, with forceful
     sway,
Drives the sharp rock; the solid beams give way,
The folds are shattered; from the crackling door
Leap the resounding bars, the flying hinges roar.
Now rushing in the furious chief appears,
Gloomy as night, and shakes two shining spears;
A dreadful gleam from his bright armour came,
And from his eye-balls flashed the living flame:
He moves a god, resistless in his course,
And seems a match for more than mortal force.
Then pouring after, thro' the gaping space
A tide of Trojans flows, and fills the place;
The Greeks behold, they tremble, and they fly,
The shore is heaped with death, and tumult rends
     the sky.

Alexander Pope (1688–1744),
from the Iliad of Homer (c. 900 BC)

A Sea-Battle

The Christian crew came on, in form of battle pight,
And like a crescent cast themselves preparing for to
    fight.
On other side the Turks, which trusted power too
    much,
Disorderly did spread their force, the will of God was
    such.
Well, at the last they met, and first with cannons'
    thunder,
Each other sought with furious force to slit their
    ships in sunder.
The barks are battered sore, the galleys galled with
    shot,
The hulks are hit and every man must stand unto his
    lot.
The powder sends his smoke into the cruddy skies,
The smoulder stops our nose with stench, the sun
    offends our eyes,
The pots of lime unslaked, from highest top are
    cast,
The parchéd peas are not forgot to make them slip as
    fast.

The wildfire-works are wrought and cast in foemen's
  face,
The grappling hooks are strechéd forth, the pikes are
  pushed apace.
The halberds hew on head, the brownbills bruise the
  bones,
The harquebus doth spit his spite, with pretty piercing
  stones.
The drums cry dub-a-dub, the braying trumpets blow,
The whistling fifes are seldom heard, these sounds do
  drown them so.
The voice of warlike wights, to comfort them that
  faint,
The piteous plaints of golden hearts, which were with
  fears attaint.
The groaning of such ghosts as gaspéd now for
  breath,
The prayers of the better sort, preparéd unto death.
And to be short, each grief which on the earth mat
  grow,
Was eath and easy to be found, upon these floods to
  flow.
If any sight on earth, may unto hell resemble,
Then sure this was a hellish sight, it makes me yet to
  tremble!

George Gascoigne (1542–77)

The War in Heaven *from* Paradise Lost

~

                    Now storming fury rose,
And clamour, such as heard in heav'n till now
Was never; arms on armour clashing brayed
Horrible discord, and the madding wheels
Of brazen chariots raged; dire was the noise
Of conflict; over head the dismal hiss
Of fiery darts in flaming volleys flew,
And flying vaulted either host with fire.
So under fiery cope together rushed
Both battles main, with ruinous assault
And inextinguishable rage; all heav'n
Resounded, and had earth been then, all earth
Had to her centre shook. What wonder? When
Millions of fierce encount'ring angels fought
On either side, the least of whom could wield
These elements, and arm him with the force
Of all their regions: how much more of power
Army against army numberless to raise
Dreadful combustion warring, and disturb,
Though not destroy, their happy native seat;
Had not the eternal King omnipotent
From His strong hold of heav'n high over-ruled

And limited their might; though numbered such,
As each divided legion might have seemed
A numerous host; in strength each armed hand
A legion; led in fight, yet leader seemed
Each warrior single as in chief, expert
When to advance, or stand, or turn the sway
Of battle, open when and when to close
The ridges of grim war; no thought of flight,
None of retreat, no unbecoming deed
That argued fear; each on himself relied,
As only in his arm the moment lay
Of victory: deeds of eternal fame
Were done, but infinite; for wide was spread
That war, and various: sometimes on firm ground
A standing fight; then, soaring on main wing,
Tormented all the air; all air seemed then
Conflicting fire.

John Milton (1608–74)

A Burnt Ship

Out of a fired ship, which, by no way
But drowning, could be rescued from the flame,
Some men leapt forth, and ever as they came
Near the foe's ships, did by their shot decay;
So all were lost, which in the ship were found.
    They in the sea being burnt, they in the burnt
      ship drowned.

John Donne (1572–1631)

Hohenlinden

~

On Linden, when the sun was low,
All bloodless lay th' untrodden snow,
And dark as winter was the flow
Of Iser, rolling rapidly:

But Linden saw another sight,
When the drum beat at dead of night,
Commanding fires of death to light
The darkness of her scenery.

By torch and trumpet fast arrayed,
Each horseman drew his battle-blade,
And furious every charger neighed,
To join the dreadful revelry.

Then shook the hills with thunder riven,
Then rushed the steed to battle driven,
And louder than the bolts of heaven,
Far flashed the red artillery.

But redder yet that light shall glow
On Linden's hills of stainéd snow,
And bloodier yet the torrent flow
Of Iser, rolling rapidly.

'Tis morn, but scarce yon level sun
Can pierce the war-clouds, rolling dun,
Where furious Frank, and fiery Hun,
Shout in their sulph'rous canopy.

The combat deepens. On, ye brave,
Who rush to glory, or the grave!
Wave, Munich! All thy banners wave,
And charge with all thy chivalry!

Few, few, shall part where many meet!
The snow shall be their winding-sheet,
And every turf beneath their feet
Shall be a soldier's sepulchre.

Thomas Campbell (1777–1844)

from A Description of the Battle in Fight

～

Some for death do call, some life desire,
Some care not, others burial require.
Some beat their breasts, as evil they had done,
Others in fiery hot revenge do burn.
Some lay, as if to hear the trumpet sound,
And others lay, as sprawling on the ground.
Some wished their death's revenge upon their foe,
Others with dying eyes their friends not know.
Some their parents, children, cried to see,
Others wished life some difference to agree.
But lovers with a soft and panting heart,
Did wish their mistress at their last depart
To shut their eyes and wounds to close,
Whose dying spirits to their mistress goes.
Foes hands into each others wounds thrust wide,
As if their hearts would pull out from each side;
Where friends in dear embracements are close twined
By their affection strong, in death they are joined.
Some wished to live, yet long for death through pain,
Others die grieving that their foe's not slain,
Or else repent what they so rash have done,
And wish the battle were to be begun.

Some gently sinking, so by fainting fall,
And quietly do yield when Death them call.
Some drunk with death, not able are to stand,
And reeling fall, struck down by Death's cold hand,
Some ling'ring long, as lovers when part must,
Others, as willing yield to fate, their dust,
And sweetly lies, as if asleep in night;
Some stern, as if new battles were to fight.
Some softly murmuring like a bubbling stream,
Yet sweetly smile in death, as in a dream,
Whose souls with soft-breathed sighs to heaven fly,
To live with gods above the starry sky.
Thus several noises through the air do ring,
And several postures Death to men doth bring.

Margaret Cavendish,
Duchess of Newcastle (1624?–74)

War's Zodiac

~

War and the sun are twins. As the sun rides
In's chariot, all of flames, which himself guides
Through heaven, the vast earth measuring in one day,
And of all countries, so, takes full survey;
Cheering all nations, which his god-like eyes,
Who sets as he sets; rise as he does rise,
And in a year this princely bridegroom shines
Twelve times, in his twelve houses, the twelve signs.

When into horned moons the squadrons change,
Then the battalia does in *Aries* range:
Here the brave van comes up – a soldier's pride –
Who die here, win a death that's dignified.

When, like two stiff-necked bulls, fell armies meet,
Being gored quite through with wounds, from head to
    feet,
The bellowing *Taurus* is a lusty sign,
That soldiers, then, in scarlet triumphs shine.

Honour and warlike anger single forth
Troops against troops, and wings to show their worth:

Men then with men, their masculine valours try,
Which makes the battle move in *Gemini*.

Hot grows the day, the strong the weaker beat;
Which seen, the wearied van with soft retreat
Gives back; and in this politic retire,
Cancer wins time to kindle fresher fire.

Lightning and thunder then bring up the rear,
And with it, Death, who plays the murderer:
Hell's fury are the marshals for the day,
For *Leo* roars and does his fangs display.

Still to be killing is a belluine rage,
The thirst of vengeance therefore to assuage.
Mercy puts forth a hand and prisoners takes,
And then mild *Virgo* from her tent awakes.

As when two dragons, breathless through deep
    wounds,
'Tis doubtful which the other's life confounds:
So, 'twixt two armies whilst coy victory hovers,
The hopes and fears of both *Libra* discovers.

Pell-mell, then to't again; the chain-shot flies
And sweeps down lanes of men, tossing i'th' skies
Armours and limbs, to show that *Scorpio* throws
His rancorous breath forth, poisoning where it goes.

O thou old English archer, *Sagittary*,
Now laughed at is the bow which thou dost carry;
Thy grey goose wing, which once brave battles won,
Hangs loose; for bullets on thy errands run.

What coward flies the field? And wounds does feign
To save himself out of war's sulphurous ruin,
For a few drops? Off is the peasant borne!
His sign shall be the skipping *Capricorn*.

Winter now comes, heaven's sluices pour out rain;
Or, fields are standing pools through armies slain:
Else a torn country swims in her own tears,
And then *Aquarius* up his standard rears.

But when pay slacks, and health with victuals gone,
Soldiers being forced to live on dry poor-John;
Yet, two by two (like sharks) themselves combine
For booties; *Pisces* is this luckless sign.

Thus home at last, the soldier comes,
As useless as the hung-up drums:
And, but by noble hands being fed,
May beg hard; hardly yet get bread.

Thomas Dekker (1570–1632)

Chapter 4

~

STAND AT EASE

After the fear, the pity; after the fearful goodbyes, the pitiful pain of coming home. Or not coming home. And then the questions, whispered throughout the poems that follow. What? When? Who? Where? and (perhaps above all) Why?

Anthem for Doomed Youth

What passing bells for these who die as cattle?
  Only the monstrous anger of the guns.
  Only the stuttering rifles' rapid rattle
Can patter out their hasty orisons.
No mockeries for them; no prayers nor bells,
  Nor any voice of mourning save the choirs, –
The shrill, demented choirs of wailing shells;
  And bugles calling for them from sad shires.

What candles may be held to speed them all?
  Not in the hands of boys but in their eyes
Shall shine the holy glimmers of goodbyes.
  The pallor of girls' brows shall be their pall;
Their flowers the tenderness of patient minds,
And each slow dusk a drawing-down of blinds.

Wilfred Owen (1893–1918)

A Wife in London

~

She sits in the tawny vapour
  That the Thames-side lanes have uprolled,
  Behind whose webby fold on fold
Like a waning taper
  The street-lamp glimmers cold.

A messenger's knock cracks smartly,
  Flashed news is in her hand
  Of meaning it dazes to understand
Though shaped so shortly:
  He – has fallen – in the far South land . . .

'Tis the morrow; the fog hangs thicker,
  The postman nears and goes:
  A letter is brought whose lines disclose
By the firelight flicker
  His hand, whom the worm now knows:

Fresh – firm – penned in highest feather –
    Page-full of his hoped return,
    And of home-planned jaunts by brake and burn
In the summer weather,
    And of new love that they would learn.

Thomas Hardy (1840–1928)

The Due of the Dead

I sit beside my peaceful hearth,
    With curtains drawn and lamp trimmed bright
I watch my children's noisy mirth;
    I drink in home, and its delight.

I sip my tea, and criticize
    The war, from flying rumours caught;
Trace on the map, to curious eyes,
    How here they marched, and there they fought.

In intervals of household chat,
    I lay down strategetic laws;
Why this manoeuvre, and why that;
    Shape the event, or show the cause.

Or, in smooth dinner-table phrase,
    'Twixt soup and fish, discuss the fight;
Give to each chief his blame or praise;
    Say who was wrong and who was right.

Meanwhile o'er Alma's bloody plain,
    The scathe of battle has rolled by –
The wounded writhe and groan – the slain
    Lie naked staring to the sky.

The out-worn surgeon plies his knife,
    Nor pauses with the closing day;
While those who have escaped with life
    Find food and fuel as they may.

And when their eyes in sleep they close,
    After scant rations duly shared,
Plague picks his victims out, from those
    Whom chance of battle may have spared.

Still when the bugle sounds the march,
    He tracks his prey through steppe and dell;
Hangs fruit to tempt the throats that parch,
    And poisons every stream and well.

All this with gallant hearts is done;
    All this with patient hearts is borne:
And they by whom the laurel's won,
    Are seldom they by whom 'tis worn.

No deed, no suffering of the war,
    But wins us fame, or spares us ill;
Those noble swords, though drawn afar,
    Are guarding English homesteads still.

Owe we a debt to these brave men,
    Unpaid by aught that's said or sung,
By leaders from a ready pen,
    Or phrases from a flippant tongue.

The living, England's hand may crown
    With recognition, frank and free;
With titles, medals, and renown;
    The wounded shall our pensioners be.

But they, who meet a soldier's doom –
    Think you, it is enough, good friend,
To plant a laurel at their tomb,
    And carve their names – and there an end?

No. They are gone: but there are left
    Those they loved best while they were here –
Parents made childless, babes bereft,
    Desolate widows, sisters dear.

All these let grateful England take:
    And, with a large and liberal heart,
Cherish for her soldier's sake,
    And of her fullness give them part.

Fold them within her sheltering breast;
    Their parent, husband, brother, prove,
That so the dead may be at rest,
    Knowing those cared for whom they love.
                    William Makepeace Thackeray (1811–63)

The Poor and Honest Soldier

When wild war's deadly blast was blawn,
    And gentle peace returning,
Wi' mony a sweet babe fatherless,
    And mony a widow mourning;
I left the lines and tented field,
    Where lang I'd been a lodger,
My humble knapsack a' my wealth,
    A poor and honest soldier.

A leal light heart was in my breast,
    My hand unstained wi' plunder,
And for fair Scotia, hame again,
    I cheery on did wander.
I thought upon the banks o'Coil,
    I thought upon my Nancy,
I thought upon the witching smile
    That caught my youthful fancy.

At length I reached the bonny glen
    Where early life I sported;
I passed the mill, and trysting thorn,
    Where Nancy aft I courted:

Wha' spied I but my ain dear maid,
    Down by her mother's dwelling!
And turned me round to hide the flood
    That in my een was swelling.

Wi' altered voice, quoth I, "Sweet lass,
    Sweet as yon hawthorn's blossom,
Oh! Happy, happy may he be,
    That's dearest to thy bosom!
My purse is light, I've far to gang,
    And fain wad be thy lodger;
I've served my king and country lang –
    Take pity on a soldier."

Sae wistfully she gazed on me,
    And lovelier was than ever;
Quo' she, "A soldier ance I loved,
    Forget him shall I never:
Our humble cot, and hamely fare,
    Ye freely shall partake it,
That gallant badge – the dear cockade –
    Ye're welcome for the sake o't."

She gazed – she reddened like a rose –
    Syne pale like ony lily;

She sank within his arms and cried,
    "Art thou my ain dear Willie?"
"By Him who made yon sun and sky,
    By whom true love's regarded,
I am the man; and thus may still
    True lovers be rewarded!"

"The wars are o'er, and I'm come hame,
    And find thee still true-hearted;
Though poor in gear, we're rich in love,
    And mair, we'se ne'er be parted."
Quo' she, "My grandsire left me gowd,
    A mailen plenished fairly;
And come, my faithful soldier lad,
    Thou'rt welcome to't dearly!"

For gold the merchant ploughs the main,
    The farmer ploughs the manor;
But glory is the soldier's prize,
    The soldier's wealth is honour:
The brave poor soldier ne'er despise,
    Nor count him as a stranger;
Remember he's his country's stay
    In day and hour of danger.

                    Robert Burns (1759–96)

from The Prelude

~

While thus I wandered, step by step led on,
It chanced a sudden turning of the road
Presented to my view an uncouth shape
So near that, slipping back into the shade
Of a thick hawthorn, I could mark him well,
Myself unseen. He was of stature tall,
Stiff in his form, and upright, lank and lean;
A man more meagre, as it seemed to me,
Was never seen abroad by night or day.
His arms were long, and bare his hands; his mouth
Showed ghastly in the moonlight: from behind,
A milestone propped him, and his figure seemed
Half-sitting and half-standing. I could mark
That he was clad in military garb,
Though faded, yet entire. He was alone,
Had no attendant, neither dog nor staff,
Nor knapsack; in his very dress appeared
A desolation, a simplicity
That seemed akin to solitude. Long time
Did I peruse him with a mingled sense
Of fear and sorrow.

William Wordsworth (1770–1850)

The Returned Soldier

The soldier, full of battles and renown,
And gaping wonder of each quiet lown,
And strange to every face he knew so well,
Comes once again in this old town to dwell.
But man alone is changed; the very tree
He sees again where once he used to swee;
And the old fields where once he tented sheep,
And the old mole-hills where he used to leap,
And the old bush where once he found a nest,
Are just the same, and pleasure fills his breast.
He sees the old path where he used to play
At chock and marbles many a summer day,
And loves to wander where he went a boy,
And fills his heart with pleasure and with joy.

John Clare (1793–1864)

To Captain Hungry

Do what you come for, Captain, with your news,
That's sit and eat; do not my ears abuse.
I oft look on false coin, to know't from true:
Not that I love it more than I will you.
Tell the gross Dutch those grosser tales of yours,
How great you were with the two emperors,
And yet are with their princes; fill them full
Of your Moravian horse, Venetian bull,
Tell them what parts you've ta'en, whence run away,
What states you've gulled, and which yet keeps you
    in pay.
Give them your services and embassies
In Ireland, Holland, Sweden (pompous lies)
In Hungary and Poland, Turkey too;
What at Leghorn, Rome, Florence, you did do;
And, in some year, all these together heaped,
For which there must more sea and land be leaped
– If but to be believed you have the hap –
Than can a flea at twice skip in the map.
Give your young statesman (that first make you
    drunk
And then lie with you, closer than a punk,

For news) your Villeroys and Silleries,
Janins, your nuncios and your Tuileries,
Your archduke's agents and your Beringhams,
That are your words of credit. Keep your names
Of Hannow, Shieter-huissen, Popenheim,
Hans-spiegel, Rotteinberg, and Boutersheim
For your next meal: this you are sure of. Why
Will you not part with them here, unthriftily?
Nay, now you puff, tusk, and draw up your chin,
Twirl the poor chain you run a-feasting in.
Come, be not angry, you are Hungry: eat;
Do what you come for, Captain, there's your meat.

Ben Jonson (1572–1640)

from The Song of Tiadatha

In the mighty British Army
Rumour is the only issue
That arrives at units larger
Than it leaves the Base Supply Park.
Up it comes without an indent
(Possibly in lieu of lime-juice)
Heaven only knows its maker;
Like a toy balloon it swells up,
Gently growing big and bigger;
At the Dump the Mr Know-Alls
Have a blow to make it fatter,
Pass it on to Transport drivers,
Who in their turn puff their hardest,
Make it change its shape a little,
Hand it over with the rations.
Then the minions of the Q.M.
Do their little bit to help it,
After which the Sergeant-Major
Takes a lusty breath to fix it,
Sends it up into the trenches
As a full-blown army rumour.

"Klip-Klip" (1919)

from Henry IV, Part Two

~

Enter Rumour, painted full of tongues
Open your ears; for which of you will stop
The vent of hearing when loud Rumour speaks?
I, from the Orient to the drooping West,
Making the wind my post-horse, still unfold
The acts commencéd on this ball of earth.
Upon my tongues continual slanders ride,
The which in every language I pronounce,
Stuffing the ears of men with false reports.
I speak of peace, while covert enmity
Under the smile of safety wounds the world;
And who but Rumour, who but only I,
Make fearful musters, and prepared defence,
While the big year, swoll'n with some other grief,
Is thought with child by the stern tyrant War,
And no such matter? Rumour is a pipe
Blown by surmises, jealousies, conjectures,
And of so easy and so plain a stop
That the blunt monster with uncounted heads,
The still-discordant multitude,
Can play upon it.

William Shakespeare (1564–1616)

To the Lord General Fairfax

~

Fairfax, whose name in arms through Europe rings,
    Filling each mouth with envy or with praise,
    And all her jealous monarchs with amaze
    And rumours loud that daunt remotest kings,
Thy firm unshaken virtue ever brings
    Victory home, though new rebellions raise
    Their Hydra heads, and the false North displays
    Her broken league to imp their serpent wings.
Oh yet a nobler task awaits thy hand;
    For what can war, but endless war still breed,
    Till truth and right from violence be freed,
And public faith cleared from the shameful brand
    Of public fraud? In vain doth valour bleed
    While avarice and rapine share the land.

John Milton (1608–74)

from Upon Appleton House: To the Lord Fairfax

From that blest bed the hero came,
Whom France and Poland yet does fame:
Who, when retired here to peace,
His warlike studies could not cease;
But laid these gardens out in sport
In the just figure of a fort;
And with five bastions it did fence,
As aiming one for every sense.

When in the east the morning ray
Hangs out the colours of the day,
The bee through these known alleys hums,
Beating the *dian* with its drums.
Then flowers their drowsy eyelids raise,
Their silken ensigns each displays,
And dries its pan yet dank with dew,
And fills its flask with odours new.

These, as their Governor goes by,
In fragrant volleys they let fly;
And to salute their Governess
Again as great a charge they press:

None for the virgin Nymph; for she
Seems with the flowers a flower to be.
And think so still! though not compare
With breath so sweet, or cheek so fair.

Well shot, ye firemen! Oh how sweet,
And round your equal fires do meet,
Whose shrill report no ear can tell,
But echoes to the eye and smell.
See how the flowers, as at parade,
Under their colours stand displayed:
Each regiment in order grows,
That of the tulip, pink, and rose.

But when the vigilant patrol
Of stars walks round about the Pole,
Their leaves, that to the stalks are curled,
Seem to their staves the ensigns furled.
Then in some flower's beloved hut
Each bee as sentinel is shut
And sleeps so too: but if once stirred,
She runs you through, nor asks the word.

Oh thou, that dear and happy isle
The garden of the world ere while,

Thou paradise of four seas,
Which heaven planted us to please,
But, to exclude the world, did guard
With watery if not flaming sword;
What luckless apple did we taste
To make us mortal, and thee waste?

Unhappy! Shall we never more
That sweet militia restore,
When gardens only had their towers,
And all the garrisons were flowers,
When roses only arms might bear,
And men did rosy garlands wear?
Tulips, in several colours barred,
Were then the Switzers of our Guard.

The gardener had the soldier's place,
And his more gentle first did trace.
The nursery of all things green
Was then the only magazine.
The winter quarters were the stoves,
Where he the tender plants removes.
But war all this doth overgrow;
We ordnance plant and powder sow.

Andrew Marvell (1621–78)

An Old Soldier of the Queen's

Of an old soldier of the Queen's,
With an old motley coat, and a malmsey nose,
And an old jerkin that's out at the elbows,
And an old pair of boots, drawn on without hose
Stuffed with rags instead of toes;
    And an old soldier of the Queen's,
    And the Queen's old soldier.

With a rusty sword that's hacked with blows,
And an old dagger to scare away the crows,
And an old horse that reels as he goes,
And an old saddle that no man knows,
    And an old soldier of the Queen's,
    And the Queen's old soldier.

With his old wounds in Eighty-Eight,
Which he recovered, at Tilbury fight;
With an old passport that never was read,
That in his old travels stood him in great stead;
    And an old soldier of the Queen's,
    And the Queen's old soldier.

With his old gun, and his bandoliers,
And an old head-piece to keep warm his ears,
With an old shirt is grown to wrack,
With a huge louse, with a great list on his back,
Is able to carry a pedlar and his pack;
   And an old soldier of the Queen's,
   And the Queen's old soldier.

With an old quean to lie by his side,
That in old time had been pockified;
He's now rid to Bohemia to fight with his foes,
And he swears by his valour he'll have better clothes,
Or else he'll lose legs, arms, fingers, and toes,
And he'll come again, when no man knows,
   And an old soldier of the Queen's,
   And the Queen's old soldier.

Anon (c. 1650)

from Isabella

The Gen'ral! one of those brave old commanders,
Who served through all the glorious wars in Flanders;
Frank and good-natured, of an honest heart,
Loving to act the steady friendly part:
None led through youth a gayer life than he,
Cheerful in converse, smart in repartee.
Sweet was his night, and joyful was his day,
He dined with Walpole, and with Oldfield lay;
But with old age its vices came along,
And in narration he's extremely long;
Exact in circumstance, and nice in dates,
He each minute particular relates.
If you name one of Marlb'ro's ten campaigns,
He tells you its whole history for your pains:
And Blenheim's field becomes by his reciting,
As long in telling as it was in fighting.
His old desire to please is still expressed;
His hat's well cocked, his periwig's well dressed:
He rolls his stockings still, white gloves he wears,
And in the boxes with the beaux appears:
His eyes through wrinkled corners cast their rays;
Still he looks cheerful, still soft things he says:

And still remembr'ing that he once was young
He strains his crippled knees, and struts along.

Sir Charles Hanbury Williams (1708–59)

The Man with the Wooden Leg

~

There was man lived quite near us;
He had a wooden leg and a goldfinch in a green cage.
His name was Farkey Anderson,
And he'd been in a war to get his leg.
We were very sad about him,
Because he had such a beautiful smile
And was such a big man to live in a very small house.
When he walked on the road his leg did not matter so
    much;
But when he walked in his little house
It made an ugly noise.
Little Brother said his goldfinch sang the loudest of
    all birds,
So that he should not hear his poor leg
And feel too sorry about it.

Katherine Mansfield (1888–1923)

The Pluralist and Old Soldier

~

A soldier maimed and in the beggars' list
Did thus address a well-fed pluralist:
SOLDIER: At Guadeloupe my leg and thigh I lost,
No pension have I, though its right I boast;
Your reverence, please some charity bestow,
Heav'n will pay me double – when you're there, you
   know.
PLURALIST: Heav'n pay me double? Vagrant, know
   that I
Ne'er give to strollers, they're so apt to lie:
Your parish and some work would you become,
So haste away – or constable's your doom.
SOLDIER: May't please your reverence, hear my case,
   and then
You'll say I'm poorer than the most of men:
When Marlboro siegéd Lisle I first drew breath,
And there my father met untimely death;
My mother followed, of a broken heart,
So I've no friend or parish, for my part.
PLURALIST: I say, begone.
     – With that he loudly knocks,
     And Timber-toe begins to smell the stocks.

~ 173 ~

Away he stumps – but in a rood or two,
He cleared his weasand and his thoughts broke
through:

SOLDIER: This 'tis to beg of those who sometimes
   preach
Calm charity, and ev'ry virtue teach;
But their disguise to common sense is thin:
A pocket buttoned – hypocrite within.
Send me, kind heav'n, the well-tanned captain's face,
Who gives me twelvepence and a curse, with grace.
But let me not in house or lane or street
These treble-pensioned parsons ever meet.
And when I die may I still numbered be
With the rough soldier, to eternity.

John Collier (1708–86)

from A Larum for London

~

I know your liberal minds will scorn t'impose
The sweat of bloody danger on the brow
Of any man, but you'll reward him for it:
He shall at least, when he hath lost his limbs,
Be sent for harbour to a spittle-house.
How say ye, shall he not? Good reason then,
But we should venture – yes, to laugh at you,
Whilst we behold the Spaniard cut your throats.
An abject, base mechanic set awork,
A sweaty cobbler, whose best industry
Is but to clout a shoe, shall have his fee;
But let a soldier that hath spent his blood,
Is lamed, diseased, or any way distressed,
Appeal for succour, then you look askance
As if you knew him not, respecting more
An ostler, or some drudge that rakes your kennels,
Than one that fighteth for the commonwealth.

Anon (1600)

The Soldier that has Seen Service

~

From Calpe's rock, with loss of leg,
Reduced from port to port to beg,
    See the conquering hero comes:
An ass's panniers bear his all,
Two sickly brats that fret and bawl,
    And suck, for want of food, their thumbs.

The drooping mother follows near,
Now heaves a sigh, now drops a tear,
    And casts the fond, maternal gaze;
Mars bluntly strives to cheat his dame,
Reminds her of his stock of fame,
    And bids her hope for better days.

"Alas," she cries, "and what is fame?
An empty sound, not worth a name.
    Doth fame the needful loaf supply?
I'd give up all the fame you boast
For one fair joint of boiled or roast,
    Or griskin fat or mutton-pie.

"Was it for this we left our home
About the troubled world to roam,
    To conquer Spain and want a meal?
Ah! Had we never bled for those
Who see our still increasing woes,
    And comfort's cup refuse to deal!"

Mars owns 'tis true, and cries, "Too late
'Tis now for us to carp at fate,
    Or call the moment back that's flown.
Let shame at length the state o'erwhelm,
That knows he fought to save the realm,
    And lets the wounded soldier moan."

"Amen," she cries; Mars wipes her tear,
Prepares some better theme to cheer,
    Of battles, songs or pleasures gone;
From knapsack takes his little store,
Hoping that time will make it more;
    Then parts his crust and hobbles on.

Anon (1788)

~

Wars now is worse than walking horse
For like a hackney tied at rack,
Old soldier so, who wanteth force,
Must learn to bear a pedlar's pack
And trudge to some good market town
So from a knight become a clown.

As good serve suiter in his shop
As follow wars, that begg'ry brings,
Nay play the child and drive the top
Or favour many fonder things,
And thrive thereby, seems better far,
Than run a-gadding to the war.

Wars wins the workman scarce his bread,
A fig for fame, if that be all,
Wars quickly gets a broken head
And gains no better fruit at all.
But when good blood is wasted out,
Into the joints wars thrusts the gout.

Lame limbs and legs, and mangled bones
Wars brings a man unwares, God wot,
With privy pangs, sad sighs and groans,
Then come to court where nought is got,
Save shales and shells when kernel sweet
The hogs have, trampling under feet.

If five and forty sons I had,
Not one to court nor wars should go,
Except that some of them were mad,
So proud both where I would or no:
But wars of all the arts that is
Stands most from hap or heaven's bliss.

Wars is a worm in conscience still,
That gnaws the guts and heart in twain.
Who goes to wars must make his will
For fear he comes not home again:
But at his welcome home indeed
He gets not words, so starves at need.

Or at court gate must sit and watch,
Like Goodman Coxcomb keeping crows,
Go supperless to bed like Patch,

Or for his lodging gauge his clothes:
A warm reward, a whip, a hood
Would do a silly fool more good.

Sell house and land to follow drum
And so bring home an empty bag,
Then like bare Tom of Bedlam come,
With broken breech and many a rag:
And see what pity world will take
On thee, for thy great service sake.

"Keep that thou hast" is counsel good,
What wars may win think that is lost,
For prince do hazard life and blood
If en'mies breathe but on this cost:
Shun other wars as from a snake
Whose sting a mortal wound will make.

Wars is but called the scourge of God,
A plague for man, and each thing's foe,
A whisking wand, a cruel rod,
That draws out blood at ev'ry blow.
A fearful bug, a cursèd fiend,
That drives good days and years to end.

If devils dance when drum doth sound,
And saints do weep where blood is shed,
If wars doth shake the heavy ground
Whereon fish, fowl and beasts are bred:
O wars pack hence and run away,
From me and all my friends this day.

For where thou goest all plagues repair,
All mischiefs march, all sorrows swim,
All filthy facts infects the air,
All sin and vice is at the brim:
All dearth and famine are afloat,
And all or most have God forgot.

Fie! Fly from wars as from a fire
That all burns up or kills in haste,
Spoils and robs all, leaves all in mire,
Consumeth all, brings all to waste:
Yet when the wars rules all like king,
Wars is himself a begg'ry thing.

But if proud wars begin to brawl
And quarrels pick to wrong our right
Then clap on arms, corslets and all,

To put a wrangling foe to flight:
And make them run like rats away,
That robs our cheese house every day.

Lo, knights, how plain poor poets shifts,
In scambling world to scour the coast,
With rhymes, and sends such New Years gifts
From sick man's couch to court in post:
Where this may make a merry head
To smile before he goes to bed.

Thomas Churchyard (1520–1604)

Faithless Nelly Gray: A Pathetic Ballad

Ben Battle was a soldier bold,
 And used to war's alarms;
But a cannon ball took off his legs,
 So he laid down his arms.

Now as they bore him off the field,
 Said he, "Let others shoot,
For here I leave my second leg,
 And the Forty-Second Foot!"

The army-surgeons made him limbs:
 Said he, – "They're only pegs:
But there's as wooden members quite
 As represent my legs!"

Now Ben he loved a pretty maid,
 Her name was Nelly Gray;
So he went to pay his devoirs
 When he'd devoured all his pay.

But when he called on Nelly Gray,
 She made him quite a scoff;

And when she saw his wooden legs,
    Began to take them off.

"O Nelly Gray, O Nelly Gray!
    Is this your love so warm?
The love that loves a scarlet coat,
    Should be more uniform!"

She said, "I loved a soldier once,
    For he was blithe and brave;
But I will never have a man
    With both legs in the grave!

"Before you had those timber toes,
    Your love I did allow,
But then, you know, you stand upon
    Another footing now!"

"O Nelly Gray, O Nelly Gray!
    For all your jeering speeches,
At duty's call I left my legs
    In Badajos's *breeches*!"

"Why then," said she, "you've lost the feet
    Of legs in war's alarms,

And now you cannot wear the shoes
  Upon your feats of arms!"

"O false and fickle Nelly Gray;
  I know why you refuse:-
Though I've no feet – some other man
  Is standing in my shoes.

"I wish I ne'er had seen your face;
  But now a long farewell!
For you will be my death; alas!
  You will not be my *Nell*!"

Now when he went from Nelly Gray,
  His heart so heavy got
And life was such a burden grown
  It made him take a knot.

So round his melancholy neck
  A rope he did entwine
And, for the second time in life,
  Enlisted in the Line.

One end he tied around a beam,
  And then removed his pegs

And as his legs were off – of course
    He soon was off his legs.

And there he hung till he was dead
    As any nail in town, –
For though distress had cut him up,
    It could not cut him down.

A dozen men sat on his corpse
    To find out why he died –
And they buried Ben in four crossroads
    With a stake in his inside.

Thomas Hood (1799–1845)

Disabled

~

He sat in a wheeled chair, waiting for dark,
And shivered in his ghastly suit of grey,
Legless, sewn short at elbow. Through the park
Voices of boys rang saddening like a hymn,
Voices of play and pleasure after day,
Till gathering sleep had mothered them from him.

About this time Town used to swing so gay
When glow-lamps budded in the light blue trees,
And girls glanced lovelier as the air grew dim,
– In the old times, before he threw away his knees.
Now he will never feel again how slim
Girls' waists are, or how warm their subtle hands,
All of them touch him like some queer disease.

There was an artist silly for his face,
For it was younger than his youth, last year.
Now, he is old; his back will never brace;
He's lost his colour very far from here,
Poured it down shell-holes till the veins ran dry,
And half his lifetime lapsed in the hot race
And leap of purple spurted from his thigh.

One time he liked a bloodsmear down his leg,
After the matches carried shoulder-high.
It was after football, when he'd drunk a peg,
He thought he'd better join. He wonders why . . .
Someone had said he'd look a god in kilts.

That's why; and maybe too to please his Meg,
Aye, that was it, to please the giddy jilts,
He asked to join. He didn't have to beg;
Smiling they wrote his lie; aged nineteen years.
Germans he scarcely thought of; and no fears
Of Fear came yet. He thought of jewelled hilts
For daggers in plaid socks; of smart salutes;
And care of arms; and leave; and pay arrears;
Esprit de corps; and hints for young recruits.
And soon, he was drafted out with drums and
    cheers.

Some cheered him home, but not as crowds cheer
    Goal.
Only a solemn man who brought him fruits
Thanked him, and then inquired about his soul.
Now, he will spend a few sick years in Institutes,
And do what things the rules consider wise,
And take whatever pity they may dole.

Tonight he noticed how the women's eyes
Passed from him, to the strong men that were
    whole.
How cold and late it is! Why don't they come
And put him to bed? Why don't they come?

Wilfred Owen (1894–1918)

"And There was a Great Calm"
(On the Signing of the Armistice, 11 Nov. 1918)

There had been years of Passion – scorching, cold,
And much Despair, and Anger heaving high,
Care whitely watching, Sorrows manifold,
Among the young, among the weak and old,
And the pensive Spirit of Pity whispered, "Why?"

Men had not paused to answer. Foes distraught
Pierced the thinned peoples in a brute-like blindness,
Philosophies that sages long had taught,
And Selflessness, were as an unknown thought,
And "Hell!" and "Shell!" were yapped at
    Lovingkindness.

The feeble folk at home had grown full-used
To "dug-outs", "snipers", "Huns", from the war-adept
In the mornings heard, and at evetides perused;
To day-dreamt men in millions, when they mused –
To nightmare-men in millions when they slept.

Waking to wish existence timeless, null,
Sirius they watched above where armies fell;

He seemed to check his flapping when, in the lull
Of night a boom came thencewise, like the dull
Plunge of a stone dropped into some deep well.

So, when old hopes that earth was bettering slowly
Were dead and damned, there sounded "War is done!"
One morrow. Said the bereft, and meek, and lowly,
"Will men some day be given to grace? yea, wholly,
And in good sooth, as our dreams used to run?"

Breathless they paused. Out there men raised their
    glance
To where had stood those poplars lank and lopped,
As they had raised it through the four years' dance
Of Death in the now familiar flats of France;
And murmured, "Strange, this! How? All firing
    stopped?"

Aye; all was hushed. The about-to-fire fired not,
The aimed-at moved away in trance-lipped song.
One checkless regiment slung a clinched shot
And turned. The Spirit of Irony smirked out, "What?
Spoil peradventures woven of Rage and Wrong?"

Thenceforth no flying fires inflamed the gray,
No hurtlings shook the dewdrop from the thorn,
No moan perplexed the mute bird on the spray;
Worn horses mused: "We are not whipped today;"
No weft-winged engines blurred the moon's thin
   horn.

Calm fell. From Heaven distilled a clemency;
There was peace on earth and silence in the sky;
Some could, some could not, shake off misery:
The Sinister Spirit sneered: "It had to be!"
And again the Spirit of Pity whispered, "Why?"

Thomas Hardy (1840–1928)

First News from Villafranca

~

Peace, peace, peace, do you say?
    What! – with the enemy's guns in our ears?
    With the country's wrong not rendered back?
What! – while Austria stands at bay
    In Mantua, and our Venice bears
    The cursed flag of the yellow and black?

Peace, peace, peace, do you say?
    And this the Mincio? Where's the fleet,
    And where's the sea? Are we all blind
Or mad with the blood shed yesterday,
    Ignoring Italy under our feet,
    And seeing things before, behind?

Peace, peace, peace, do you say?
    What! – uncontested, undenied?
    Because we triumph, we succumb?
A pair of Emperors stand in the way,
    (One of whom is a man, beside)
To sign and seal our cannons dumb?

No, not Napoleon! – he who mused
    At Paris, and at Milan spake,
    And at Solferino led the fight:
Not he we trusted, honoured, used
    Our hope and hearts for … till they break –
    Even so, you tell us … in his sight.

Peace, peace, is still your word?
    We say you lie then! That is plain.
    There *is* no peace, and shall be none.
Our very dead would cry "Absurd!"
    And clamour that they died in vain,
    And whine to come back to the sun.

Hush! more reverence for the dead!
    They've done the most for Italy
    Evermore since the earth was fair.
Now would that we had died instead,
    Still dreaming peace meant liberty,
    And did not, could not mean despair.

Peace, you say? – yes, peace in truth!
    But such a peace as the ear can achieve
    'Twixt the rifle's click and the rush of the ball,

'Twixt the tiger's spring, and the crunch of the
     tooth,
  'Twixt the dying atheist's negative
  And God's face – waiting, after all!
          Elizabeth Barret Browning (1806–61)

Afterwards

～

"My King and Country needed me," to fight
    The Prussian's tyranny.
I went and fought, till our assembled might
With a wan triumph had dispersed in flight
    At least the initial P.

I came back. In a crowded basement now
    I scratch, a junior clerk.
Each day my tried experience must bow
Before the callow boy, whose shameless brow
    Usurps my oldtime work.

I had not cared – but that my toil was vain,
    But that still rage the strong:
I had not cared – did any good remain.
But now I scratch, and wait for war again,
    Nor shall I need to wait long.
                H.B.K. Allpass (d. 1916)

Chapter 5

FALL OUT

What can anyone say? Many of the poems in this final section enact the struggle to speak of the days that were, and of the impossible necessity of remembering. Now the drums beat a slower rhythm, and we can only end where we began, on the beach, on a "barren strand" with "dark water tumbling on the shore" . . .

from Morte D'Arthur

~

So all day long the noise of battle rolled
Among the mountains by the winter sea;
Until King Arthur's table, man by man,
Had fallen in Lyonnesse about their lord,
King Arthur: then, because his wound was deep,
The bold Sir Bedivere uplifted him,
Sir Bedivere, the last of all the knights,
And bore him to a chapel nigh the field,
A broken chancel with a broken cross,
That stood on a dark strait of barren land.
On one side lay the ocean, and on one
Lay a great water, and the moon was full.

    Then spake King Arthur to Sir Bedivere:
"The sequel of today unsolders all
The goodliest fellowship of famous knights
Whereof this world holds record. Such a sleep
They sleep – the men I loved. I think that we
Shall never more, at any future time,
Delight our souls with talk of knightly deeds,
Walking about the gardens and the halls
Of Camelot, as in the days that were."

Alfred Lord Tennyson (1809–92)

~ 198 ~

Dirge for Two Veterans

∽

The last sunbeam
Lightly falls from the finished Sabbath,
On the pavement here, and there beyond it is looking
    Down a new-made double grave.

Lo, the moon ascending,
Up from the east the silvery round moon,
Beautiful over the house-tops, ghastly, phantom
    moon,
    Immense and silent moon.

I see a sad procession,
And I hear the sound of coming full-keyed bugles,
All the channels of the city streets they're flooding,
    As with voices and with tears.

I hear the great drums pounding,
And the small drums steady whirring,
And every blow of the great convulsive drums,
    Strikes me through and through.

For the son is brought with the father,
(In the foremost ranks of the fierce assault they fell,
Two veterans son and father dropt together,
	And the double grave awaits them).

Now nearer blow the bugles,
And the drums strike more convulsive,
And the daylight o'er the pavement quite has faded,
	And the strong dead-march enwraps me.

In the eastern sky up-buoying,
The sorrowful vast phantom moves illumined,
('Tis some mother's large transparent face,
	In heaven brighter growing).

O strong dead-march you please me!
O moon immense with your silvery face you soothe
	me!
O my soldiers twain! O my veterans passing to burial!
	What I have I also give you.

The moon gives you light,
And the bugles and the drums give you music,
And my heart, O my soldiers, my veterans,
	My heart gives you love.

				Walt Whitman (1819–92)

Dirge for a Soldier

Close his eyes; his work is done.
What to him is friend or foeman,
Rise of moon or set of sun,
Hand of man or kiss of woman?

Lay him low, lay him low,
In the clover or the snow.
What cares he? He cannot know.
Lay him low!

As man may, he fought his fight,
Proved his truth by his endeavour:
Let his sleep in solemn night,
Sleep for ever and for ever.

Fold him in his country's stars,
Roll the drum and fire the volley!
What to him are all our wars?
What but death bemocking folly?

Leave him to God's watching eye:
Trust him to the hand that made him.
Mortal love weeps idly by:
God alone has power to aid him.

Lay him low, lay him low,
In the clover or the snow.
What cares he? He cannot know.
Lay him low!
George Henry Broker (1823–90)

The Burial of Sir John Moore after Corunna

Not a drum was heard, not a funeral note,
    As his corse to the rampart we hurried;
Not a soldier discharged his farewell shot
    O'er the grave where our hero we buried.

We buried him darkly at dead of night,
    The sods with our bayonets turning,
By the struggling moonbeam's misty light
    And the lanthorn dimly burning.

No useless coffin enclosed his breast,
    Not in sheet or in shroud we wound him;
But he lay like a warrior taking his rest
    With his martial cloak around him.

Few and short were the prayers we said,
    And we spoke not a word of sorrow;
But we steadfastly gazed on the face that was dead,
    And we bitterly thought of the morrow.

We thought, as we hollowed his narrow bed
    And smoothed down his lonely pillow,
That the foe and the stranger would tread o'er his
      head,
    And we far away on the billow!

Lightly they'll talk of the spirit that's gone,
    And o'er his cold ashes upbraid him –
But little he'll reck, if they let him sleep on
    In the grave where a Briton has laid him.

But half of our heavy task was done
    When the clock struck the hour for retiring;
And we heard the distant and random gun
    That the foe was sullenly firing.

Slowly and sadly we laid him down,
    From the field of his fame fresh and gory;
We carved not a line, and we raised not a stone,
    But we left him alone with his glory.

Charles Wolfe (1791–1823)

The Forced Recruit: Solferino 1859

In the ranks of the Austrian you found him,
  He died with his face to you all;
Yet bury him here where around him
  You honour your bravest that fall.

Venetian, fair-featured and slender,
  He lies shot to death in his youth,
With a smile on his lips over-tender
  For any mere soldier's dead mouth.

No stranger, and yet not a traitor,
  Though alien the cloth on his breast,
Underneath it how seldom a greater
  Young heart, has shot sent to rest!

By your enemy tortured and goaded
  To march with them, stand in their file,
His musket (see) never was loaded,
  He facing your guns with that smile!

As orphans yearn on to their mothers,
  He yearned to your patriot bands; –

"Let me die for our Italy, brothers,
    If not in your ranks, by your hands!

"Aim straightly, fire steadily, spare me
    A ball in the body which may
Deliver my heart here, and tear me
    This badge of the Austrian away!"

So thought he, so died he this morning.
    What then? Many others have died.
Ay, but easy for men to die scorning
    The death-stroke, who fought side by side –

One tricolor floating above them;
    Struck down 'mid triumphant acclaims
Of an Italy rescued to love them
    And blazon the brass with their names.

But he – without witness or honour,
    Mixed, shamed in his country's regard,
With the tyrants who march in upon her,
    Died faithful and passive: 'twas hard.

'Twas sublime. In a cruel restriction
    Cut off from the guerdon of sons,

With most filial obedience, conviction,
   His soul kissed the lips of her guns.

That moves you? Nay, grudge not to show it,
   While digging a grave for him here:
The others who died, says your poet,
   Have glory, – let *him* have a tear.
      Elizabeth Barret Browning (1806–61)

Do Not Weep

~

Do not weep, maiden, for war is kind.
Because your lover threw wild hands towards the sky
And the affrighted steed ran on alone,
Do not weep
War is kind.

    Hoarse, booming drums of the regiment,
    Little souls who thirst for fight,
    These men were born to drill and die,
    The unexplained glory flies above them,
    Great is the battle-god, great, and his kingdom –
    A field where a thousand corpses lie.

Do not weep, babe, for war is kind.
Because your father tumbled in the yellow trenches,
Raged at his breast, gulped and died,
Do not weep
War is kind.

    Swift blazing flag of the regiment,
    Eagle with crest of red and gold,
    These men were born to drill and die.

Point for them the virtue of slaughter,
Make plain to them the excellence of killing
And a field where a thousand corpses lie.

Mother whose heart hung humble as a button
On the bright splendid shroud of your son,
Do not weep.
War is kind.

Stephen Crane (1871–1900)

The Tears of Scotland. Written in the Year 1746

Mourn, hapless Caledonia, mourn
Thy banished peace, thy laurels torn!
Thy sons, for valour long renowned,
Lie slaughtered on their native ground;
Thy hospitable roofs no more
Invite the strangers to the door;
In smoky ruins sunk they lie,
The monuments of cruelty.

The wretched owner sees afar
His all become the prey of war;
Bethinks him of his babes and wife,
Then smites his breast, and curses life,
Thy swains are famished on the rocks,
Where once they fed their wanton flocks:
Thy ravished virgins shriek in vain;
Thy infants perish on the plain.

What boots it then, in every clime,
Through the wide-spreading waste of time,
Thy martial glory, crowned with praise,
Still shone with undiminished blaze?

Thy tow'ring spirit now is broke,
Thy neck is bended to the yoke.
What foreign arms could never quell
By civil rage and rancour fell.

The rural pipe and merry lay
No more shall cheer the happy day:
No social scenes of gay delight
Beguile the dreary winter night:
No strains but those of sorrow flow,
And naught be heard but sounds of woe,
While the pale phantoms of the slain
Glide nightly o'er the silent plain.

Oh, baneful curse, oh, fatal morn,
Accursed to ages yet unborn!
The sons against their fathers stood,
The parents shed his children's blood.
Yet when the rage of battle ceased
The victor's soul was not appeased;
The naked and forlorn must feel
Devouring flames, and murd'ring steel.

The pious mother doomed to death
Forsaken, wanders o'er the heath.

The bleak wind whistles round her head
Her helpless orphans cry for bread;
Bereft of shelter, food, and friend,
She views the shades of night descend,
And, stretched beneath th'inclement skies,
Weeps o'er her tender babes, and dies.

While the warm blood bedews my veins,
And unimpaired remembrance reigns,
Resentment of my country's fate
Within my filial breast shall beat;
And, spite of her insulting foe,
My sympathizing verse shall flow:
"Mourn, hapless Caledonia, mourn
Thy banished peace, thy laurels torn."

Tobias Smollett (1721–71)

In Flanders Fields

~

In Flanders fields the poppies blow
Between the crosses, row on row,
  That mark our place; and in the sky
  The larks, still bravely singing, fly
Scarce heard amid the guns below.

We are the Dead. Short days ago
We lived, felt dawn, saw sunset glow,
  Loved and were loved, and now we lie
    In Flanders fields.

Take up our quarrel with the foe:
To you from failing hands we throw
  The torch; be yours to hold it high.
  If ye break faith with us who die
We shall not sleep, though poppies grow
    In Flanders fields.

John McCrae (1872–1918)

To the Memory of Sir Henry Ellis
Who Fell in the Battle of Waterloo

Weep'st thou for him, whose doom was sealed
On England's proudest battlefield?
For him, the lion-heart, who died
In victory's full resistless tide?
      Oh, mourn him not!
By deeds like his that field was won,
And fate could yield to valour's son
      No brighter lot.

He heard his band's exulting cry,
He saw the vanquished eagles fly;
And envied be his death of fame,
It shed a sunbeam o'er his name
      That nought shall dim:
No cloud obscured his glory's day,
It saw no twilight of decay –
      Weep not for him!

And breathe no dirge's plaintive moan,
A hero claims far loftier tone!
Oh, proudly should the war-song swell,

Recording how the mighty fell
        In that dread hour,
When England, 'midst the battle-storm –
The avenging angel – reared her form
        In tenfold power.

Yet gallant heart! To swell thy praise,
Vain were the minstrel's noblest lays;
Since he, the soldier's guiding star,
The victor-chief, the lord of war,
        Has owned thy fame:
And oh! Like *his* approving word,
What trophied marble could record
        A warrior's name?

Felicia Hemans (1793–1835)

Epitaph upon Captain Bourcher
Late Slain in the Wars in Zeeland

~

Fie, Captains, fie! Your tongues are tied too close,
Your soldiers eke by silence purchase shame:
Can no man pen in metre nor in prose,
The life, the death, the valiant acts, the fame,
The birth, behaviour, nor the noble name
Of such a fere as you in fight have lost?
Alas such pains would quickly quite the cost.

Bourcher is dead, whom each of you did know,
Yet no man writes one word to paint his praise,
His sprite on high, his carcass here below,
Do both condemn your doting idle days:
Yet cease they not to sound his worthy ways,
Who lived to die, and died again to live,
With death dear bought, he did his death forgive.

He might for birth have boasted noble race,
Yet were his manners meek and always mild,
Who gave a guess by gazing on his face,
And judged thereby might quickly be beguiled:
In field a lion and in town a child,

Fierce to his foe, but courteous to his friend.
Alas the while, his life so soon should end?

To serve his prince his life was ever pressed,
To serve his God, his death he thought but due,
In all attempts as forward as the best,
And all too forwards which we all may rue,
His life so showed, his death eke tried it true:
For where God's foes in thickest press did stand,
Bourcher caught bane with bloody sword in hand.

And mark the courage of a noble heart,
When he in bed lay wounded wondrous sore,
And heard alarm, he soon forgot his smart,
And called for arms to show his service more:
"I will to field," quoth he, "and God before."
Which said, he sailed into more quiet coast,
Still praising God, and so gave up the ghost.

Now muse not, reader, though we stones can speak,
Or write sometimes the deeds of worthy ones,
I could not hold although my heart should break
Because here by me buried are his bones,
But I must tell this tale thus for the nonce.

When men cry mum and keep such silence long,
Then stones must speak, else dead men shall have
  wrong.

George Gascoigne (1542–77)

The Dead

~

Blow out, you bugles, over the rich dead!
　　There's none of these so lonely and poor of old,
　　But, dying, has made us rarer gifts than gold.
These laid the world away; poured out the red
Sweet wine of youth; gave up the years to be
　　Of work and joy; and that unhoped serene,
　　That men call age; and those who would have
　　　　been,
Their sons, they gave, their immortality.

Blow, bugles, blow! They brought us, for our dearth,
　　Holiness, lacked so long, and love, and pain.
Honour has come back, as a king, to earth,
　　And paid his subjects with a royal wage;
And nobleness walks in our ways again;
　　And we have come into our heritage.
　　　　　　　　　　　Rupert Brooke (1887–1916)

The Soldier's Death

Trail all your pikes, dispirit every drum,
March in a slow procession from afar,
Ye silent, ye dejected men of war!
Be still the hautboys, and the flute be dumb!
Display no more, in vain, the lofty banner.
For see, where on the bier before ye lies
The pale, the fall'n, th'untimely sacrifice
To your mistaken shrine, to your false idol Honour.

Anne Finch, Countess of Winchilsea (d. 1720)

A Christmas Ghost-Story

South of the Line, inland from far Durban,
A mouldering soldier lies – your countryman.
Awry and doubled up are his grey bones,
And on the breeze his puzzled phantom moans
Nightly to clear Canopus: "I would know
By whom and when the All-Earth-gladdening Law
Of Peace, brought in by that Man Crucified,
Was ruled to be inept, and set aside?
And what of logic or of truth appears
In tacking 'Anno Domini' to the years?
Near twenty-hundred liveried thus have hied,
But tarries yet the Cause for which He died."

Thomas Hardy (1840–1928)

Hushed be the Camps Today

Hushed be the camps today,
And soldiers let us drape our war-torn weapons
And each with musing soul retire to celebrate
Our dear commander's death.

No more for him life's stormy conflicts,
Nor victory, nor defeat – no more time's dark events,
Charging like ceaseless clouds across the sky.

But sing poet in our name,
Sing of the love we bore him – because you, dweller in
    the camps, know it truly.

As they invault the coffin there,
Sing – as they close the doors of earth upon him –
    one verse,
For the heavy hearts of soldiers.

Walt Whitman (1819–92)

from Ode on the Death of the Duke of Wellington

Who is he that cometh, like an honoured guest,
With banner and with music, with soldier and with
     priest,
With a nation weeping, and breaking on my rest?
Mighty seaman, this is he
Was great by land as thou by sea.
Thine island loves thee well, thou famous man,
The greatest sailor since our world began.
Now, to the roll of muffled drums
To thee the greatest soldier comes;
For this is he
Was great by land as thou by sea.
His foes were thine; he kept us free;
O give him welcome, this is he
Worthy of our gorgeous rites,
And worthy to be laid by thee;
For this is England's greatest son,
He that gained a hundred fights,
Nor ever lost an English gun;
This is he that far away
Against the myriads of Assaye
Clashed with his fiery few and won;

And underneath another sun,
Warring on a later day,
Round affrighted Lisbon drew
The treble works, the vast designs
Of his laboured rampart-lines,
Where he greatly stood at bay,
Whence he issued forth anew,
And ever great and greater grew,
Beating from the wasted vines
Back to France her banded swarms,
Back to France with countless blows,
Till o'er the hills her eagles flew
Beyond the Pyrenean pines
Followed up in valley and glen
With blare of bugle, clamour of men,
Roll of cannon and clash of arms,
And England pouring on her foes.
Such a war had such a close.
Again their ravening eagle rose
In anger, wheeled on Europe-shadowing wings,
And barking for the thrones of kings;
Till one that sought but Duty's iron crown
On that loud sabbath shook the spoiler down;
A day of onsets of despair!
Dashed on every rocky square
Their surging charges foamed themselves away;

Last, the Prussian trumpet blew;
Thro' the long tormented air
Heaven flashed a sudden jubilant ray,
And down we swept and charged and overthrew.
So great a soldier taught us there,
What long-enduring hearts could do
In that world-earthquake, Waterloo!
Mighty seaman, tender and true,
And pure as he from taint of craven guile,
O saviour of the silver-coasted isle,
O shaker of the Baltic and the Nile,
If aught of things that here befall
Touch a spirit among things divine,
If love of country move thee there at all,
Be glad, because his bones are laid by thine!
And thro' the centuries let a people's voice
In full acclaim,
A people's voice,
The proof and echo of all human fame,
A people's voice, when they rejoice
At civic revel and pomp and game,
Attest their great commander's claim
With honour, honour, honour, honour to him
Eternal honour to his name.

Alfred Lord Tennyson (1809–92)

A Satirical Elegy on the Death of a
Late Famous General

His Grace? Impossible! What, dead?
Of old age, too, and in his bed!
And could that Mighty Warrior fall?
And so inglorious, after all!
Well, since he's gone, no matter how,
The last loud trump must wake him now:
And, trust me, as the noise grows stronger,
He'd wish to sleep a little longer.
And could he be indeed so old
As by the newspapers we're told?
Threescore, I think, is pretty high;
'Twas time in conscience he should die.
This world he cumbered long enough;
He burnt his candle to the snuff;
And that's the reason, some folks think,
He left behind *so great a stink*.
Behold his funeral appears,
Nor widow's sighs, nor orphan's tears,
Wont at such times each heart to pierce,
Attend the progress of his hearse.
But what of that, his friends may say,

He had those honours in his day.
True to his profit and his pride,
He made them weep before he died.

Come hither, all ye empty things,
Ye bubbles raised by breath of kings;
Who float upon the tide of state,
Come hither, and behold your fate.
Let pride be taught by this rebuke:
How very mean a thing's a Duke;
From all his ill-got honours flung,
Turned to that dirt from whence he sprung.

Jonathan Swift (1667–1745)

from Childe Harold's Pilgrimage

Stop! – for thy tread is on an Empire's dust!
　　An earthquake's spoil is sepulchred below!
　　Is the spot marked with no colossal bust?
　　Nor column trophied for triumphal show?
　　None; but *the moral's truth* tells simpler so. –
　　As the ground was before, thus let it be; –
　　How that red rain hath made the harvest grow!
　　And is this all the world has gained by thee,
Thou first and last of Fields, king-making Victory?

And Harold stands upon this place of skulls,
　　The grave of France, the deadly Waterloo!
　　How in an hour the Power which gave annuls
　　Its gifts, transferring fame as fleeting too! –
　　In "pride of place" here last the Eagle flew,
　　Then tore with bloody talon the rent plain,
　　Pierced by the shaft of banded nations through;
　　Ambition's life and labours all were vain –
He wears the shattered links of the world's broken
　　chain.

　　　　　　George Gordon, Lord Byron (1788–1824)

The Battle of Blenheim

〜

It was a summer evening,
    Old Kaspar's work was done,
And he before his cottage door
    Was sitting in the sun,
And by him sported on the green
His little grandchild Wilhelmine.

She saw her brother Peterkin
    Roll something large and round,
Which he beside the rivulet
    In playing there had found;
He came to ask what he had found,
That was so large, and smooth, and round.

Old Kaspar took it from the boy,
    Who stood expectant by;
And then the old man shook his head,
    And, with a natural sigh,
"'Tis some poor fellow's skull," said he,
"Who fell in the great victory.

"I find them in the garden,
    For there's many here about;
And often when I go to plough,
    The ploughshare turns them out!
For many thousand men," said he,
"Were slain in the great victory."

"Now tell us what 'twas all about,"
    Young Peterkin, he cries;
And little Wilhelmine looks up
    With wonder-waiting eyes;
"Now tell us all about the war
And what they fought each other for."

"It was the English," Kaspar cried,
    "Who put the French to rout;
But what they fought each other for,
    I could not well make out;
But everybody said," quoth he,
"That 'twas a famous victory.

"My father lived at Blenheim then,
    Yon little stream hard by;
They burnt his dwelling to the ground,
    And he was forced to fly;

So with his wife and child he fled,
Nor had he where to rest his head.

"With fire and sword the country round
    Was wasted far and wide,
And many a childing mother, then,
    And new-born baby died;
But things like that, you know, must be
At every famous victory.

"They say it was a shocking sight
    After the field was won;
For many thousand bodies here
    Lay rotting in the sun;
But things like that, you know, must be
After a famous victory.

"Great praise the Duke of Marlbro' won,
    And our good Prince Eugene."
"Why 'twas a very wicked thing!"
    Said little Wilhelmine.
"Nay . . . nay . . . my little girl," quoth he,
"It was a famous victory.

"And everybody praised the Duke
     Who this great fight did win."
"But what good came of it at last?"
     Quoth little Peterkin.
"Why that I cannot tell," said he,
"But 'twas a famous victory."
                    Robert Southey (1774–1843)

Epitaph on Benjamin Tremlyn,
an old soldier, buried in Bremhill Churchyard
at the age of 92

A poor old soldier shall not lie unknown,
Without a verse, and this recording stone.
'Twas his in youth o'er distant lands to stray,
Danger and death companions of his way.
Here in his native village, drooping age
Closed the lone evening of his pilgrimage.
Speak of the past, of names of high renown,
Or his brave comrades long to dust gone down,
His eye with instant animation glowed,
Though ninety winters on his head had snowed.
His country, whilst he lived, a boon supplied,
And faith her shield held o'er him when he died;
Hope, Christian, that his spirit lives with God,
And pluck the wild weeds from his lowly sod,
Where, dust to dust, beside the chancel's shade,
Till the last trumpet sounds, a brave man's bones
    are laid.

William Lisle Bowles (1762–1850)

After the Soldier's Funeral

And so we hide our dead in silent shade,
And hasten back to life, and life's parade;
Plunge into duty, grind in labor's mill,
Till the eye sees not, and the heart is still;
Weep each reverse and shout each victory,
And breathe our benisons, dear flag, on thee.
Living or dying, nation of the free,
Our hopes, our hearts, our lives, are all with thee.

Samuel Francis Smith (1808–95)

The Night-March

With banners furled, and clarions mute,
    An army passes in the night;
And beaming spears and helms salute
    The dark with bright.

In silence deep the legions stream,
    With open ranks, in order true;
Over boundless plains they stream and gleam –
    No chief in view!

Afar, in twinkling distance lost,
    (So legends tell) he lonely wends
And back through all that shining host
    His mandate sends.

Herman Melville (1819–91)

"When you see millions of the mouthless dead"
~

When you see millions of the mouthless dead
Across your dreams in pale battalions go,
Say not soft things as other men have said,
That you'll remember. For you need not so.
Give them not praise. For, deaf, how should they
    know
It is not curses heaped on each gashed head?
Nor tears. Their blind eyes see not your tears flow.
Nor honour. It is easy to be dead.
Say only this, "They are dead." Then add thereto,
"Yet many a better one has died before."
Then, scanning all the o'ercrowded mass, should you
Perceive one face that you loved heretofore,
It is a spook. None wears the face you knew.
Great death has made all his for evermore.

Charles Hamilton Sorley (1895–1915)

The Beleaguered City

I have read, in some old marvellous tale,
    Some legend strange and vague,
That a midnight host of spectres pale
    Beleaguered the walls of Prague.

Beside the Moldau's rushing stream,
    With the wan moon overhead,
There stood, as in an awful dream,
    The army of the dead.

White as a sea-fog, landward bound,
    The spectral camp was seen,
And, with a sorrowful, deep sound,
    The river flowed between.

No other voice nor sound was there,
    No drum, nor sentry's pace;
The mist-like banners clasped the air,
    As clouds with clouds embrace.

But, when the old cathedral bell
    Proclaimed the morning prayer,

The white pavilions rose and fell
    On the alarméd air.

Down the broad valley fast and far
    The troubled army fled;
Up rose the glorious morning star,
    The ghastly host was dead.

I have read, in the marvellous heart of man,
    That strange and mystic scroll,
That an army of phantoms vast and wan
    Beleaguer the human soul.

Encamped beside Life's rushing stream,
    In Fancy's misty light,
Gigantic shades and shadows gleam
    Portentous through the night.

Upon its midnight battle-ground
    The spectral camp is seen,
And, with a sorrowful, deep sound,
    Flows the River of Life between.

No other voice nor sound is there,
    In the army of the grave,

No other challenge breaks the air,
But the rushing of Life's wave.

And, when the solemn and deep church-bell,
Entreats the soul to pray,
The midnight phantoms feel the spell,
The shadows sweep away.

Down the broad Vale of Tears afar
The spectral camp is fled;
Faith shineth as a morning star,
Our ghastly fears are dead.
William Wadsworth Longfellow (1807–82)

To L.H.B. (1894–1915)

⁓

Last night for the first time since you were dead
I walked with you, my brother, in a dream.
We were at home again beside the stream
Fringed with tall berry bushes, white and red.
"Don't touch them: they are poisonous," I said.
But your hand hovered, and I saw a beam
Of strange, bright laughter flying round your head
And as you stooped I saw the berries gleam.
"Don't you remember? We called them Dead Man's
    Bread!"
  I woke and heard the wind moan and the roar
Of the dark water tumbling on the shore.
Where – where is the path of my dream for my eager
    feet?
By the remembered stream my brother stands
Waiting for me with berries in his hands . . .
"These are my body. Sister, take and eat."

Katherine Mansfield (1888–1923)

from The Revolt of Islam

~

The spear transfixed my arm that was uplifted
    In swift expostulation, and the blood
Gushed round its point. I smiled, and, "Oh! thou
        gifted
    With eloquence which shall not be withstood,
    Flow thus!" I cried in joy, "thou vital flood,
Until my heart be dry, ere thus the cause
    For which thou wert aught worthy to be
        subdued –
Ah, ye are pale, – ye weep, – your passions pause, –
'Tis well! ye feel the truth of love's benignant laws.

"Soldiers, our brethren and our friends are slain.
    Ye murdered them, I think, as they did sleep!
Alas, what have ye done? the slightest pain
    Which ye might suffer, there were eyes to weep,
    But ye have quenched them – there were smiles
        to steep
Your hearts in balm, but they are lost in woe;
    And those whom love did set his watch to keep
Around your tents, truth's freedom to bestow,
Ye stabbed as they did sleep – but they forgive ye now.

"Oh wherefore should ill ever flow from ill,
    And pain still keener pain for ever breed?
We all are brethren – even the slaves who kill
    For hire, are men; and to avenge misdeed
    On the misdoer, doth but Misery feed
With her own broken heart! O Earth, O Heaven!
    And thou, dread Nature, which to every deed
And all that lives or is, to be hath given,
Even as to thee have these done ill, and are forgiven!

"Join then your hands and hearts, and let the past
    Be as a grave which gives not up its dead
To evil thoughts." – A film then overcast
    My sense with dimness, for the wound, which
        bled
    Fresh, swift shadows o'er mine eyes had shed.
When I awoke, I lay mid friends and foes,
    And earnest countenances on me shed
The light of questioning looks, whilst one did
        close
My wound with balmiest herbs, and soothed me to
    repose.

And one whose spear had pierced me, leaned
    beside,
    With quivering lips and humid eyes; – and all
Seemed like some brothers on a journey wide
    Gone forth, whom now strange meeting did
    befall
    In a strange land, round one whom they might
    call
Their friend, their chief, their father, for assay
    Of peril, which had saved them from the thrall
Of death, now suffering. Thus the vast array
Of those fraternal bands were reconciled that day.

Percy Bysshe Shelley (1792–1822)

Strange Meeting

It seemed that out of the battle I escaped
Down some profound dull tunnel, long since scooped
Through granites which Titanic wars had groined,
Yet also there encumbered sleepers groaned,
Too fast in thought or death to be bestirred.
Then, as I probed them, one sprang up, and stared
With piteous recognition in fixed eyes,
Lifting distressful hands, as if to bless.
And by his smile, I knew that sullen hall;
With a thousand fears that vision's face was grained;
Yet no blood reached there from the upper ground,
And no guns thumped, or down the flues made moan.
"Strange friend," I said, "here is no cause to mourn."
"None," said the other, "save the undone years,
The hopelessness. Whatever hope is yours,
Was my life also; I went hunting wild
After the wildest beauty in the world,
Which lies not calm in eyes, or braided hair,
But mocks the steady running of the hour,
And if it grieves, grieves richlier than here.
For by my glee might many men have laughed,
And of my weeping something had been left,

Which must die now. I mean the truth untold,
The pity of war, the pity war distilled.
Now men will go content with what we spoiled.
Or, discontent, boil bloody, and be spilled.
They will be swift with swiftness of the tigress,
None will break ranks, though nations trek from
   progress.
Courage was mine, and I had mystery;
Wisdom was mine, and I had mastery;
To miss the march of this retreating world
Into vain citadels that are not walled.
Then, when much blood had clogged their chariot-
   wheels,
I would go up and wash them from sweet wells.
Even with truths that lie too deep for taint.
I would have poured my spirit without stint
But not through wounds; not on the cess of war.
Foreheads of men have bled where no wounds were.
I am the enemy you killed, my friend.
I knew you in this dark; for so you frowned
Yesterday through me as you jabbed and killed.
I parried; but my hands were loath and cold.
Let us sleep now . . ."

Wilfred Owen (1893–1918)

The Man he Killed

"Had he and I but met
　　By some old ancient inn,
We should have sat us down to wet
　　Right many a nipperkin!

"But ranged as infantry,
　　And staring face to face,
I shot at him as he at me,
　　And killed him in his place.

"I shot him dead because –
　　Because he was my foe,
Just so: my foe of course he was;
　　That's clear enough; although

"He thought he'd 'list, perhaps,
　　Off-hand like – just as I –
Was out of work – has sold his traps –
　　No other reason why.

"Yes; quaint and curious war is!
You shoot a fellow down
You'd treat if met where any bar is,
Or help to half-a-crown."

Thomas Hardy (1840–1928)

Lines Composed in Recollection of the
Expedition of the French into Russia, 1812

~

Humanity, delighting to behold
A fond reflection of her own decay,
Hath painted Winter like a shrunken, old,
And close-wrapped traveller, through the weary day
Propped on a staff, and limping o'er the plain,
As though his weakness were disturbed by pain;
Or, if a juster fancy should allow
An undisputed symbol of command,
The chosen sceptre in a withered bough,
Infirmly grasped within a palsied hand.
This emblem suits the helpless and forlorn;
But mighty Winter the device shall scorn;
For he it was – dread Winter! – who beset,
Flinging round van and rear his ghastly net,
That host, – when from the regions of the Pole
They shrunk, insane ambition's barren goal,
That host, – as huge and strong as e'er defied
Their God, and placed their trust in human pride!
As fathers persecute rebellious sons,
He smote the blossoms of the warlike youth;
He called on frost's inexorable tooth

Life to consume in manhood's firmest hold;
Nor spared the reverend blood that feebly runs;
For why – unless for liberty enrolled,
And sacred home – ah, why should hoary age be
      bold?

    Fleet the Tartar's reinless steed, –
But fleeter far the pinions of the wind,
Which from Siberia's caves the monarch freed,
And sent him forth, with squadrons of his kind,
And bade the snow their ample backs bestride,
      And to the battle ride, –
No pitying voice commands a halt, –
No courage can repel the dire assault, –
Distracted, spiritless, benumbed, and blind,
Whole legions sink, – and, in an instant, find
Burial and death: look for them – and descry
When morn returns, beneath the clear blue sky
A soundless waste, a trackless vacancy!

             William Wordsworth (1770–1850)

from The Vanity of Human Wishes

~

    On what foundation stands the warrior's pride?
How just his hopes let Swedish Charles decide:
A frame of adamant, a soul of fire,
No dangers fright him, and no labours tire;
O'er love, o'er fear, extends his wide domain,
Unconquered lord of pleasure and of pain;
No joys to him pacific sceptres yield,
War sounds the trump, he rushes to the field;
Behold surrounding kings their pow'rs combine,
And one capitulate, and one resign.
Peace courts his hand, but spreads her charms in vain;
"Think nothing gained," he cries, "till nought remain
On Moscow's walls till Gothic standards fly,
And all is mine beneath the polar sky."
The march begins in military state,
And nations on his eye suspended wait;
Stern famine guards the solitary coast,
And winter barricades the realms of frost;
He comes, nor want nor cold his course delay; —
Hide, blushing glory, hide Pultowa's day:
The vanquished hero leaves his broken bands,
And shows his miseries in distant lands;

Condemned a needy supplicant to wait;
While ladies interpose, and slaves debate.
But did not chance at length her error mend?
Did no subverted empire mark his end?
Did rival monarchs give the fatal wound?
Or hostile millions press him to the ground?
His fall was destined to a barren strand;
A petty fortress, and a dubious hand;
He left the name, at which the world grew pale,
To point a moral or adorn a tale.

Samuel Johnson (1709–84)

from The Atheist's Tragedy

Walking next day upon the fatal shore,
Among the slaughtered bodies of their men,
Which the full-stomached sea had cast upon
The sands, it was m'unhappy chance to light
Upon a face, whose favour when it lived
My astonished mind informed me I had seen.
He lay in's armour as if that had been
His coffin, and the weeping sea, like one
Whose milder temper doth lament the death
Of him whom in his rage he slew, runs up
The shore, embraces him, kisses his cheek,
Goes back again, and forces up the sands
To bury him, and every time it parts
Sheds tears upon him, till at last, as if
It could no longer endure to see the man
Whom it had slain, yet loath to leave him, with
A kind of unresolved, unwilling pace,
Winding her waves one in another, like
A man that folds his arms or wrings his hands
For grief, ebbed from the body and descends,
As if it would sink down into the earth
And hide itself for shame of such a deed.

Cyril Tourneur (c. 1575–1627)

Dover Beach

The sea is calm tonight.
The tide is full, the moon lies fair
Upon the straits; – on the French coast, the light
Gleams, and is gone; the cliffs of England stand,
Glimmering and vast, out in the tranquil bay.
Come to the window, sweet is the night-air!

Only, from the long line of spray
Where the ebb meets the moon-blanched land,
Listen! You hear the grating roar
Of pebbles which the waves draw back, and fling,
At their return, up the high strand,
Begin, and cease, and then again begin,
With tremulous cadence slow, and bring
The eternal note of sadness in.

Sophocles long ago
Heard it on the Ægean, and it brought
Into his mind the turbid ebb and flow
Of human misery; we
Find also in the sound a thought,
Hearing it by this distant northern sea.

The Sea of Faith
Was once, too, at the full, and round earth's shore
Lay like the folds of a bright girdle furled;
But now I only hear
Its melancholy, long, withdrawing roar,
Retreating to the breath
Of the night-wind down the vast edges drear
And naked shingles of the world.

Ah, love, let us be true
To one another! For the world, which seems
To lie before us like a land of dreams,
So various, so beautiful, so new,
Hath really neither joy, nor love, nor light,
Nor certitude, nor peace, nor help for pain;
And we are here as on a darkling plain
Swept with confused alarms of struggle and flight
Where ignorant armies clash by night.

Matthew Arnold (1822–88)

from A "B.E.F." Alphabet

Z is for ZERO, the time we go over,
Most of us wish we were way back in Dover,
Making munitions and living in clover
And far, far away from the trenches.

Anon (1917)

Acknowledgements

The editor and publishers gratefully acknowledge the following for their permission to reprint copyright material:

"Vitaï Lampada" by Sir Henry Newbolt, reproduced by kind permission of Peter Newbolt.

"Soldier's Dream" from *The Collected Poems of Wilfred Owen* by Wilfred Owen, edited by C. Day Lewis, published by Chatto & Windus. Used by permission of the Random House Group Limited.